TWINS of GENIUS

Mark Twain and George W. Cable, 1884

TWINS of GENIUS

by

Guy A. Cardwell

THE MICHIGAN STATE COLLEGE PRESS

1953

TO

Ethel Parmele Cardwell

TABLE of CONTENTS

PREFACE

THE LETTERS collected in this volume provide notes for chapters in the lives of Mark Twain and George W. Cable, especially from the summer of 1881 through February, 1885, the period of their chief intimacy. Because the letters alone furnish a very incomplete history of the relations between the two writers, the Introduction adds explanatory materials and a commentary on the personal and literary results of the association.

Eighteen letters from Twain to Cable and twenty letters from Cable to Twain, ranging in time from July, 1881, through October, 1906, are printed here. Although this edition of the correspondence is made up primarily of letters from the Cable Collection at the Howard-Tilton Memorial Library of the Tulane University of Louisiana, seven letters by Cable are added from the papers of the Mark Twain Estate; also printed here are one telegram and two notes written on postal cards by Cable, a letter from Twain to J. B. Pond, a letter from Pond to Twain, four letters by Mrs. Clemens, and one letter by Mrs. George Warner. Other letters, some of which either have not been published or have not been accurately published, are quoted in part in the Introduction or in headnotes to the letters.

Additional letters are extant that relate to the joint tour made by Twain and Cable, but those that I know of are in private hands, and I have not been able to secure permission to print them.

I have tried to present a faithful text of each letter, except that I have not reproduced erasures, words struck over, and the occasional abbreviations in dates of letters that would require special typography to duplicate. Other than giving the names of towns, I have omitted place names (e. g., "Paradise Road") from headings, and I have not copied printed letterheads. Some of the letters in the Cable Collection are holograph; others are typewritten copies. Copies have been collated with originals when originals were available in the Mark Twain papers. Most of the letters were accurately dated by the writers; the few dates that I have supplied or revised are printed within brackets. The arrangement of the letters is chronological.

Although the Letters, with headnotes and footnotes, may be read separately, the Introduction supplies information that clarifies details and points up biographical and literary implications. I have not thought it necessary to furnish systematic cross references for so small a book. I have, however, tried to make the book useful for reference purposes by preparing a List of Letters and an Index of Persons.

For aid in preparing this book I am especially indebted to Professors Vladimir Jelinek and William A. Ringler, Jr., who read the Introduction critically; to Dr. Garland Taylor, who made the resources of the Howard-Tilton Memorial Library available to me; to Miss Gertrude Ruhnka, who collated copies of the letters against orginals in the Mark Twain papers; to Mrs. Marion Mooney, who copied materials from newspapers; to Mrs. Jeanne Tims and Mrs. Mary Gallatin, who gave valuable secretarial assistance; and to a number of helpful librarians, including Miss Margaret A. Flint, of Springfield, Illinois, Miss Betty Copeland, of Burlington, Iowa, Mr. Karl Kiedaisch, Jr., of Keokuk, Iowa, Miss Florence M. Davison, of Evanston, Illinois, and Mr. Jules Bazin, of Montreal. I owe thanks and acknowledgments for permissions to publish manuscript materials to the officials of Tulane University, Harvard University, the New York Public Library, and the Mark Twain Estate and I am indebted to Mrs. Lucy Cable Bikle for authorization to publish letters by her father. I am grateful, too, for a research grant from the committee in charge of the Midwestern Studies Fund of Michigan State College.

ii

The usual acknowledgments for brief quotations from published works are made in footnotes, but I wish to make here, in addition, special acknowledgment of the use of certain copyrighted matter:

Harper and Brothers for excerpts from *Mark Twain's Letters* (1917), *The Love Letters of Mark Twain* (1949), *Mark Twain in Eruption* (1940), and from *My Father, Mark Twain,* by Clara Clemens (1931).

Harper and Brothers (copyright 1910) and Mildred Howells and John Mead Howells (copyright 1938) for excerpts from *My Mark Twain,* by William Dean Howells.

Charles Scribner's Sons for excerpts from *George W. Cable: His Life and Letters,* by Lucy C. Bikle (1928).

Little, Brown and Company for excerpts from *Mark Twain, Business Man,* by Samuel Charles Webster (1946).

INTRODUCTION

I. Two Novelists and Their Letters

IN THE spring of 1881 George W. Cable took his wife, a sickly woman, and their four little girls out of the steaming heat of New Orleans and established them for the summer at Franconia, in the White Mountains. Within two years' time Cable had shot from almost complete obscurity full into the public eye as the best of southern writers of fiction and as possibly the most promising of the younger American novelists.

Cable had knocked at the editorial doors of northern magazines since 1872, assisted at first by the young journalist Edward King, who had been sent into the but recently Confederate states by *Scribner's Monthly* to collect information for articles later printed as *The Great South*. Cable's "'Sieur George," published in 1873, was followed by additional short stories and by two books: *Old Creole Days* (1879), collected tales; and *The Grandissimes* (1880), a novel. *Madame Delphine,* a novelette, appeared in *Scribner's Monthly* for May, June, and July, 1881, and was published as a separate volume almost immediately.

Before returning from New Hampshire to New Orleans to work that long summer on his "History and Present Condition of New Orleans" for inclusion in the report of the Tenth Census, Cable improved "the greatest holiday" of his life by visiting in Springfield, Newport, Hartford, and New York. He had been to the North twice before, in the summers of 1875 and 1880, but this third visit was a kind of triumphal progress during which he cemented a friendship with Richard Watson Gilder and met John Hay, St. Gaudens, Charles Dudley Warner and his brother George, Harriet Beecher Stowe, William Dean Howells, and a host of other celebrities.

When he reached Hartford for a week end with the Warners, these new friends "telegraphed at once to Mr. Clemens (Mark Twain) to come up—from somewhere beyond New

1

Haven." This Twain did, bringing his wife along on the first train that left after they received the telegram. "And so I met Mark Twain. We all lunched together & 'Mark' & Mr. Warner were ever so funny."[1] This was on Monday, June 13.

At the time of this first meeting, Samuel L. Clemens, at forty-six, was a world figure, famous as a lecturer and humorous writer. Among his works already in print were *Innocents Abroad, Roughing It, The Gilded Age* (with Warner), *Old Times on the Mississippi,*[2] *Tom Sawyer,* and *The Prince and the Pauper.* He had lectured in America and in Europe and was considered a personage wherever he went. Kings and prime ministers, gold miners and hotel porters had read his books and had been pleased to know him, or to shake his hand, or merely to glimpse him in passing. Cable had just caught the attention of the public with his two fresh, promising volumes. Although his thinking on questions of race and caste had taken on a liberal bias in the 1860's, he was not yet marked as a forthright, vocal advocate of civil rights for the Negro and had not yet been widely attacked by southerners

[1] All footnotes appear at the back of the volume.

for the nonconformist views which were soon to make him notorious and obnoxious among them. He was, however, already a controversial figure, for he had antagonized the Creoles of Louisiana by portraying certain of them as speaking a delightful but broken English and as being gifted with a levity and eccentricity of character that contrasted with the more solid, reliable, and intellectually respectable qualities of Anglo-Saxons.

Yet, even in New Orleans, much if not most opinion was favorable to Cable in 1881. He shed luster on the South, and he might have developed into a favorite son. Universities and historical societies were eager for him to address them. Outside of the South his work was praised everywhere. English critics liked him. The New York *Times* pronounced *The Grandissimes* "a wonderful romance," the Boston *Journal* called its author "a novelist of positive originality," and the Baltimore *Gazette* declared him to show "the genius of a novelist of the first rank."[3] A note from William Dean Howells indicates the warmth with which he was received by northern men of letters: "Those Hartford people made me furious with their praises of you. I hate to see people foolish about a man, even if he is a great artist and every way charming."[4]

It must have seemed at the time that Cable stood at the threshold of a brilliant career and that Twain, who was customarily thought of as a wonderful, popular comic writer, but one of restricted range, had reached or passed his peak. Twain's actual achievement was grotesquely underestimated, and he still had before him part of *Life on the Mississippi,* the major part of *The Adventures of Huckleberry Finn,* his best short stories, and the less important works, *A Connecticut Yankee in King Arthur's Court* and *Joan of Arc.* Cable, surprisingly enough, was finished as a writer of serious fiction, although he drudged through thirteen more volumes of little if varying worth, the last published in 1918.

Following this initial meeting in 1881, a friendship developed very quickly between Twain and Cable, culminating in and nearly exploding during their joint lecture tour in 1884-85. The letters that the two writers exchanged are of considerable general interest; they contain lively passages that are not for the specialist alone. Set in the context of the friendship and against the background of the tour, they add valuable details to the standard picture of Twain and depth and color to the rather flatly conventional official portrait of Cable.

Twain's great eminence as a public personality made him constantly newsworthy, and by 1884 Cable was a center of controversy. As a consequence an astonishing lot was written concerning the two men and their performances while they traveled about the country together, and it has been possible to put together an extended account of this episode in the annals of entertainment in America.[5] One might think it difficult to have presented to the public a more incongruous pair than the tiny, precise, pious Cable and the shambling, disheveled, profane Clemens; but important affinities lay deep below the surface, and there was more than a joke concealed in the phrase "Twins of Genius," under which they were sometimes billed.

II. Lectures and Readings

THE VOGUE for public lectures spread rapidly in the United States after 1826, when Josiah Holbrook, of Derby, **Connecticut**, inaugurated the "lyceum" system for discussions, readings, and debates. By 1834 nearly three thousand local lyceum groups were meeting in town halls, "opera" houses, theaters, and churches. As railroads spread their network beyond the Alleghenies in the 1850's, the Middle West was opened up for professional lecturers.

Twain may have had his thoughts first turned toward lecturing by Artemus Ward in December, 1863, while he was a reporter on the *Territorial Enterprise,* of Virginia City, Nevada. Ward (Charles F. Browne), on a transcontinental lecture tour, stopped in Virginia City to lecture. He found the company there so congenial that he remained for three weeks of roistering with Sam Clemens and his friends. Shortly after this, Clemens, assisting at a church benefit in Carson City, made what has been called "really his first public appearance" when he addressed the meeting of a burlesque "Third House" of the Nevada legislature.[6] Twain's real career as a lecturer started, however, on October 25, 1866, at San Francisco, when he lectured upon his recent trip to the Hawaiian Islands. This talk he repeated across California, into Nevada, and, the following year, in New York. He lectured, too, back home in Hannibal, in St. Louis, Keokuk, and Quincy.

Addresses, lectures, and lecture tours followed at frequent intervals after Twain returned in 1867 from the excursion on the *Quaker City* that he commemorated in *Innocents Abroad.* James Redpath, owner of the Boston Lyceum Bureau, managed successful tours for him in 1868-69 and in 1871-72. During visits to England, Twain often spoke at dinners, and the public lectures he gave were eagerly applauded. The most far-flung of his tours was, of course, the world tour of 1895-96 that followed his bankruptcy.

4

The idea for a joint tour was a familiar one to Twain long before he knew Cable. In 1867 Thomas Nast proposed that he and Twain should go on the road together; in 1869 Twain proposed to Petroleum V. Nasby (D. R. Locke) that they tour together all the way to California; and in 1877 Twain went back to Nast with the suggestion that he should read while Nast did illustrative sketches.[7] Like some of Twain's other projects, this idea for a cooperative tour developed in time grandiose and impossible ramifications. For a number of months he cherished a plan for renting a private railway car, hiring a chef, and luxuriously setting out in company with William Dean Howells, Thomas Bailey Aldrich, Charles Dudley Warner, Cable, and Joel Chandler Harris. He intended to pay his co-performers fixed salaries; the risk would be his. He envisioned the expedition as a delightful and extended picnic which would be, incidentally, a glorious financial success. This ambitious project, for a "circus," or "menagerie," as Twain called it, dwindled finally, to his joint tour with Cable.

As a rule Twain was repelled by the prospect of returning to the lecture platform, with or without a companion. But even in 1883-85, a period when his books were selling phenomenally and his reputation soared, he needed money. He liked to live lavishly, and his speculations were a severe and constant drain. James R. Osgood, his publisher for *Life on the Mississippi,* had urged him to get out on the road with selections from that book. Now, as his own publisher, Twain decided to do for himself and for the forthcoming *Adventures of Huckleberry Finn* what he had not done for Osgood.

Choice of Cable as a partner was not an unreasonable one. By the time the tour began Cable had been successful as a professional reader and lecturer for parts of two seasons. Twain, sometimes extraordinarily impulsive, could have selected a much less able associate. Indeed, he not only wanted Joel Chandler Harris as a member of his menagerie, but in 1882 he rashly requested that incurably shy individual to nerve himself to a joint lecture tour.[8] Perhaps the origin of the tour with Cable should be traced back to 1882, when Twain extended the acquaintance begun in 1881 by calling on Cable in New Orleans in the spring and by entertaining him in Hartford in the autumn. It seems probable that in New Orleans he first encouraged Cable, then untried as a speaker, to attempt the platform as a regular source of income. He definitely offered a place in the menagerie to him.

In 1882 Roswell Smith of the *Century Magazine*, was also urging Cable to train himself for a part-time career as reader and lecturer. Cable had given up his secretaryship in the cotton exchange in New Orleans in October, 1881, and had no regular source of income. Industrious, canny, and impecunious, he was not difficult to persuade. After testing himself by giving the chief address at commencement exercises at the University of Mississippi in June, 1882, he wrote to Twain that his first speech in public was a success.[9] In this letter he exaggerated his ability to make his light tenor voice carry and neglected to mention the hostile reaction of the audience to his views on the South. After this initial effort Cable spoke at least once in New Orleans. Then, in March, 1883, he delivered a series of five lectures at the Johns Hopkins University, following the lecture series with three readings from his own works. At this juncture Twain arranged for Cable to give a reading in Hartford, which took place on April 4, 1883, and began seriously to promote a joint tour.[10]

Cable continued to break ground in his new profession. On June 15, 1883, he delivered an address on "The Due Restraints and Liberties of Literature" at the commencement exercises of the "Academical Department of the University of Louisiana." After that he took lessons in "elocution" for months, scored a success with his first reading,[11] and filled engagements in New York state, in New England, in Kentucky, and as far west as Chicago. On June 18, 1884, he delivered a notable, highly controversial address, a version of "The Freedman's Case in Equity,"[12] before the Alabama Historical Society, at Tuscaloosa. When Twain was finally ready to make a concrete offer through Major J. B. Pond, Cable was in a position to demand a substantial stipend. Indeed, in 1884, a lean year, Cable seems to have been one of Pond's two chief supports, for Pond's letterhead advertised that he was sole manager for Henry Ward Beecher's lectures and for George W. Cable's readings.

James Burton Pond (1838-1903), business manager for the joint tour, following in Redpath's footsteps, became the best known "impresario" of his period. Born in New York State and reared in the Middle West, he left the farm to become a printer and newspaper editor. During the Civil War he rose to a lieutenancy in the Third Wisconsin Cavalry, and after the war he was commissioned a major. In partnership with another member of Redpath's staff, he bought the Lyceum Bureau in 1875 but moved in 1879 from Boston to New York, where he opened an office of his own. He seems to have had the pliant but persistent disposition necessary to do business with Twain. Twain made use of him, abused him, and bullied him, but clung to him for years. And although he laughed at Pond, particularly when Pond became obsessed with the idea that he, too, could lecture, Twain liked him. The worst that Twain, in a calm mood, wrote of Pond is probably represented in a letter to Howells, who was contemplating a tour under Pond's management. He commented elaborately on Pond's idiocy and inability to tell the truth, Pond being afflicted not at all with George Washington's infirmity. But even in this letter Twain acknowledged an affection for his manager and a liking for his society.[13]

A somewhat kindlier judgment of Pond is contained in another letter, one written following Howells' tour:

If you got half as much as Pond prophesied, be content and praise God it has not happened to another. But I am sorry he didn't go with you; for it is marvelous to hear him yarn. He is good company, cheery and hearty, and his mill is never idle....[14]

Considering the fact that 1884, was, according to Twain, one of a series of dull years for lecturers, Pond deserved congratulations for contributing to the success of the tour. Of course, he had wonderful drawing cards in the readers he billed as his "Twins of Genius."[15]

III. Business Matters

FINANCIAL arrangements for the tour were made following active negotiations that extended over several weeks. Twain had a passion for detailed calculations and for controlling any enterprise he engaged in. When in a sanguine mood he was boundlessly optimistic, ready to assume unusual monetary risks. In this instance he decided to pay Cable a guaranteed cash amount each week, to pay Pond a percentage for managing the tour, and to gamble on his own returns. The financial details have been variously reported[16] but seem to have worked out as follows.

Twain, in proposing that Pond should manage the joint tour on a percentage basis, suggested also that Pond approach Cable with a tentative offer of $350.00 a week, all expenses paid. Pond informed Cable of the proposals, following out Twain's wishes in a half-hearted way and putting Cable on guard with equivocal expressions:

Of course this [tour] would be a very strong attraction, & I would very much like to handle it, but I certainly am not the person to advise you as my interest is your interest. . . . Once in a double team & well broke in a horse never pulls as well single after that. . . . Think and be wise. Your life is not half spent.[17]

In this same letter, Pond indicated that he had talked with Twain about at least one of Cable's peculiarities, saying, "I hear he won't travel Sundays." Twain, according to Pond, answered reflectively, "Well, I guess I shall meet him in Heaven finally. I had some fears on the subject."

Cable obviously expressed no enthusiasm at this first offer, for on July 9 Pond wrote again,[18] calling for a definite answer by July 15 and saying that Twain would rather give Cable $450.00 a week and expenses than tour with anyone else. In this letter Pond implied that he considered the new proposal an advantageous one. He pointed out that the tour would make Cable known all over the country as an entertainer and would pay very well:

8

It would net you $6,750 and me $2,259.00 but I would have to pay my whole expenses, which would be a thousand dollars. I would charge Mark 10% on the net for handling the business, & would make him pay my expenses of R. R. but not hotel bills.

The jocular, bumbling major, a user and creator of verbal saws, now urged from his experience of twelve years that "a certainty has averaged better than an uncertainty." Cable answered in a lost telegram which must have asked whether Pond had more than a tentative offer to make, and Pond replied on July 11 that the offer held good: "It is $100 pr week better than his first offer."[19]

Cable now accepted this offer of $450.00 a week, and Twain requested "Charley" Webster to work with Pond in drawing up a contract. Webster was the husband of Twain's niece, Annie Moffett, manager of Twain's publishing business, and, to his grief, Twain's general handyman. Although Twain hated routine and the details of business, he felt that no one could handle arrangements with judgment and acumen equal to his own; and he often sent out a stream of instructions, as likely as not contradictory, to men working with or for him. In his letter of July 15 to Webster[20] he set down a numbered list of points to be covered in the contract.

The tour would start after the fourth of November, election day, and the readers would appear in small towns six to ten times before they would be called on to face a metropolitan audience. The tour would run through February, with a holiday of about ten days at Christmas. Pond would employ Cable, paying him an additional $60.00 for each matinee after the second in a week, and would take care of his expenses. Pond would accompany the tour at all times except that he might send his brother, Ozias W. Pond, when unable to be with the tour himself. (These two provisions caused complications later.) Pond's additional responsibilities would include everything coming under the head of business: halls, route, printing, and prices. Indeed, once preliminary arrangements were concluded, the enterprise would be Pond's, said Twain, but added that Pond should turn profits over to him

9

daily and should send Webster daily or weekly a detailed account of receipts and disbursements.

Twain asked, also, that the itinerary be arranged to place him in Canada on December 18, 19, and 20 so that he could secure copyright there for his new book, *Huck Finn,* at the same time that it appeared in the United States; then he reconsidered and, supposing that Webster might not have his desired minimum 40,000 prepublication orders for *Huck* in hand, required that the route be planned to take him to Canada towards the end of January.

On July 22 Twain wrote to Webster approving in general a draft of the contract as submitted by Webster and Pond, recommending a few minor changes, and offering in connection with the clause dealing with Cable's expenses, facetious remarks that, viewed in the light of later events, contain elements of irony:

> In Cable's case, of course "expenses" merely means his food, lodging & transportation; & so it may be as well to use those words instead of "all" expenses. If he should become unmanageable & go to thrashing people, I should not want to have to pay his daily police court expenses. And it will be just like him to do that.[21]

He insisted, likewise, on another cautious clause: "The substitute for Pond ought to be somebody who can be changed, for another, upon complaint from Cable or me. No complaint is likely to be made, but a body can't tell."[22]

Pond had most, but not all, of the reading engagements settled before the tour began. On November 15 Clemens wrote to his brother Orion that he knew of only two dates open in January and that the New York office might have filled them.[23] On January 18 he wrote to his wife that Ozias Pond had just received a few new dates from New York.[24]

Twain's business propositions, like those of his own Colonel Sellers, frequently had an element of the fantastically magnificent about them. His actual earning power was impressive. It overawed men like Pond, dazzled journalists, and, in conjunction with his roseate dreams, left Twain himself bemused, floating on air, pinching himself to make sure that it was real. When handling large sums he often had a feeling of openhanded, careless benevolence that contrasted sharply with an equally characteristic suspicion that his associates were all bunglers and robbers.

Much of the wide public attention that the tour attracted focused on the supposedly superb cash returns. On May 14, 1885, the *Transcript* (Boston) and the *Evening Journal* (Boston) both noted that the reading tour was said to have netted Twain "nearly $35,000." The *World* (New York) for May 17 reported that Twain admitted netting $35,000 from the tour, and the newspaper assumed that Cable netted the same amount. The *Times-Democrat* (New Orleans) for December 24, 1884, asserted that Cable was earning "at the rate of $50,000 per annum out of his readings."

These estimates appear to be grossly inaccurate. On February 14, exactly fourteen days before the tour ended, Charles Webster sent a financial report to his "Uncle Sam." Pond had paid to him $673.30 for the week ending on January 31;[25] $1,279.53 for the week ending on February 7;[26] and $14,168.50 since the beginning of the tour.[27] Perhaps the tour netted Clemens about $17,000.00. And the money that Twain earned by the tour was as chaff in the wind. Like his other earnings and his wife's inheritance, it was dissipated in ill-advised speculations.

The money that Cable earned by his readings was not squandered, one may be sure, but it was not, perhaps, a totally unmixed blessing. Constant lecturing may have had something to do with his deterioration as an artist. Undoubtedly the money he made from lecturing and writing had much to do with the bitter, jealous carpings of southerners like Paul H. Hayne and Charles Gayarré, who, after the Civil War, were destitute. These proud chevaliers felt doubly betrayed when a man whom they regarded as a social inferior made money by attacking their cultural ideals, ideals that were perhaps especially precious to these unsuccessful men of letters because they constituted their one remaining claim to superior status. Although he was not without defenders, probably no southerner was so widely and sincerely hated in the South as was Cable. If he had remained a starving clerk in the office of a cotton broker, he might have been less obnoxious to his fellow southerners.

IV. The Tour

DURING the autumn of 1884 Clemens gave energetic attention to the heated campaign for the Presidency waged by James G. Blaine and Grover Cleveland. Unlike most of his acquaintances he supported Cleveland, holding then and later that Blaine was unfit for the office. He argued for his point of view with Howells and other Republican friends, presided at mass meetings, and made speeches so rhetorically effective that they were quoted and even applauded by papers supporting each of the rival parties. On November 4 he cast his vote for Cleveland; and on Wednesday, November 5, he and Cable, with Major Pond hovering in attendance, opened their joint tour in New Haven.

Their program did not always remain the same. Though Cable nearly always limited himself to Creole songs and to passages from *Dr. Sevier*, he did very occasionally vary his offerings with excerpts from "Posson Jone'," *The Grandissimes*, and possibly from other stories. Twain often made substitutions and was conscientious about offering a new bill when they read twice in the same town. Two hours was the time generally allowed for the readings; but, according to Twain, Cable expanded and drew out his offerings as the days went on. As a consequence, Twain was moved to cut the number and length of Cable's selections.

The more or less standard program began with short readings by Cable and Clemens: "Richling's Visit to Kate Riley" and "King Sollermun." Then Cable would read "Kate Riley and Ristofalo," "Narcisse in Mourning for Lady Byron," and "Mary's Night Ride." Clemens had the final place on the program, presenting as a rule his "Tragic Tale of a Fishwife," "A Trying Situation," and "A Ghost Story."[28] As the tour went on, it became normal for Cable to substitute Creole songs for one of his proposed selections.

12

Among Twain's many substitute readings were "How Come a Frenchman Doan' Talk Like a Man?," an account of the freeing of Jim by Tom and Huck, "The Jumping Frog of Calaveras County," "A Desperate Encounter with an Interviewer," a short yarn about a Governor Gardiner, a recital of difficulties with the German language, how a stammerer was cured by whistling, and "His Grandfather's Old Ram."

This last piece, taken from *Roughing It,* Ch. 12, is of special interest in that it is the only selection extant both as printed and approximately as Twain modified it for reading. On October 10, 1907, Twain dictated the story as he remembered delivering it, with the "obstructing preciseness and formalities" of the published version gone out of it.[29]

That all of Cable's most frequently used selections came from one book is a little surprising, but *Dr. Sevier* had just appeared in twelve installments in the *Century,* ending in the October issue, had been released in book form in September, was a favorite with its author, and needed advertising. Moreover, the controversial character of Cable's ideas had now become well known, and *Dr. Sevier* was itself a discussion piece. The strife over it began in southern newspapers even before the novel appeared in book form. On July 28, 1884, the New Orleans *Picayune* greeted the August issue of the *Century* with a long review of the still incomplete *Dr. Sevier.*

The *Picayune,* a liberal newspaper, had been friendly to Cable over a period of years. Now its reviewer praised Cable as an artist but took him to task for his treatment of the Creoles, for his attitude towards the Negro, and for his ideas on the moral issues of the War. The reviewer defended the Creoles against the implication that they resembled in character and language Narcisse, who though "not the hero of the story" nevertheless "furnished its most buoyant element." It was a mistake, the reviewer believed also, for Cable to affect the philosophic habit: he had too much the courage of opinions rashly reached. Probably the reviewer was fortified in this belief by repercussions following the addresses Cable made at Tuscaloosa just a few weeks earlier and at Oxford, Mississippi, in June, 1882. He would have been incited, too, by unpleasantly heterodox passages in "Who Are the Creoles" and in "The Convict Lease System in the Southern States," articles that appeared in the *Century* for January, 1883, and for February, 1884.

We have been occasionally somewhat amused, and, we confess, a little indignant, at reports that have reached us of some of Mr. Cable's deliverances at the seats of Southern learning where his reputation as a novelist has secured him audience. He seems to have been under the impression that it was his mission to preach progress to the most thoughtful and erudite men of this section, and he has done it, we understand, with wonderful *aplomb*. If we are not misinformed Mr. Cable is not only convinced that African slavery was in itself, and in its effects, evil and only evil, but that Southern civilization has still further concessions to make, which it is as yet unwilling to make, to the negro race. A Southern man afflicted with that view of the situation may win a reputation for liberalism with a certain order of minds, ignorant at once of the negro's past and present. But nothing is more easily demonstrable than that slavery was a means of progress so far as the elevation of the negro was concerned; and nothing is more certain than that it would still be a great misfortune to the negro to be forced into undue political prominence.

One particular passage in *Dr. Sevier* was like a red flag to southern readers in general. The reviewer quoted it, analyzed it, and foreswore its sentiments:

Mr. Cable does go beyond his province in *Dr. Sevier* when, after describing the march of a column of Federal soldiers through the streets of New York, "singing the song of John Brown's Body," he says in a tone of lyric exultation, "Yea, so, soldiers of the Union—though that little mother there weeps, but does not wave, as the sharp-eyed man notes well through his tears—yet, even so, yea, all the more, go 'marching on,' saviors of the Union; your cause is just. Lo, now, since nigh twenty-five years have passed, we of the South can say it!

> 'And yet—and yet, we cannot forget—'
> and we would not."

Now, it is quite true that the Southern people are content within the re-established Union, and it is equally true that they would oppose to the uttermost a second attempt to secede on the part of any Southern State. The war was fought over a ques-

14

tion of disputed interpretation of constitutional law. . . . Time has healed the wounds of war, and the waving corn is growing over fields that once were red with carnage. The Union is peace to-day, and so let it be forever! But no misery of the past, no happiness of the present, has ever led, or can ever lead, the Southern people to a confession of treason. They are not before the bar of history pleading for leniency upon sentimental grounds.

Other southern newspapers were more powerfully affected. The conservative Tuscaloosa *Gazette*, which had denounced Cable earlier, licked its chops over the plight of the *Picayune* and reprinted a portion of that paper's review to show "that George W. was 'souring' on their hands and that his Southern admirers were not altogether as progressive as to go 'marching on' with the modern George Washington and the ancient Benjamin Butler singing the song that 'John Brown's body lies a mouldering in the ground.' " The history of the world affords no parallel to the patriotism of the people of the South, declared the *Gazette*. Deserters (naming them) can be counted on one hand.

The young men will not be unworthy of the memory of their sires, many of whose bones have bleached on the hill-sides of Pennsylvania, Maryland, Virginia, Kentucky and Tennessee.— And the women of the South would look with contempt on the craven spirit who would bend the knee and prate of negro equality that "thrift may follow fawning."

Cable answered criticism briefly in the *Century* for November and, perhaps in part because of the emotional climate, chose to select readings from *Dr. Sevier*.

Olivia Clemens went down to New Haven for the opening night to wish the men well and to give Sam courage for the chore ahead of him. Except for one or two days, from this time until the two readers took a short holiday to be with their families at Christmas, they had a full schedule.

Major Pond did his advance work effectively before the reading in New Haven. Advertisements appeared in the *Daily Morning Journal and Courier* for November 3 through 5, and on the fifth a squib under "Entertainments" announced that the two "gifted humorists" would appear that evening at the Opera House, where a large and refined audi-

15

ence would doubtless welcome them. On the following day a critic announced that all of the selections of the two men were rare and finely rendered and that the entertainment was a success in every particular.

The polishing of the readings begun in New Haven was continued in other small towns, including Lowell, Springfield, and Melrose, Massachusetts. Apparently some of these early performances were rather uncertain ones. Writing from Lowell on November 12, Mark reported to Livy on a poor reading in Springfield on November 7.[30]

Twain's recollections, often inaccurate, confirm this particular impression of the moment. Dictating notes for his autobiography in October, 1907, he declared that after a long period of deserved prosperity on the part of lecturers, speculators and money-makers killed the lecture field dead about 1874. Then came ten years of "happy and holy" silence, after which he and Cable had the difficult task of facing untrained audiences. Moreover, Twain himself was green at the job. Believing that all he needed to do was to get out on the platform and read from the book, he did just that and made a botch of it. After a week's experience, he put the book aside and delivered his pieces from memory. Gradually the pieces transformed themselves into "flexible talk."[31]

The reading in Melrose on the night of November 10 was reported at length in the Boston *Morning Journal* on the following day. This, the second entertainment offered that season by the Melrose Lyceum, attracted a crowd so large that extra seats had to be moved into the hall. The critic considered the styles of the two readers to be excellently complementary and described Twain's humor as "purely American." He sketched Twain's platform manner but gave more attention to Cable, the newcomer. Twain, he wrote, came "slowly forward upon the stage, his shoulders slightly stooping, his head inclined forward, and his face unwrinkled with any trace of a smile, but bearing exactly that semi-solemn expression which one would expect to see in a man who could so seriously be-fool a foreign guide intent on showing 'Christopher Columbus on a bust.' " Cable came on the stage with easy grace, responding to the warm welcome with a pleasing smile. In contrast to Twain, who rarely varied his tone and who used few gestures, Cable "is now here, now there, now standing, now sitting, and all the time his quick, flexible, light voice is pouring out sentence after sentence of Creole dialect, emphasized by appropriate flowing gestures."

The two men gave their first joint reading in a big city on November 13, playing in Boston's Music Hall to "a very large audience" that applauded frequently. Cable gave selections from *Dr. Sevier*. Clemens read from *Huck Finn,* told of his struggles with the German language, and described his adventures with the young woman at Lucerne.[32] Howells, who attended the reading with his wife and daughter, immediately wrote one of his most enthusiastic letters to Clemens:

> You are a great artist, and you do this public thing so wonderfully well that I don't see how you could ever bear to give it up. I thought that the bits from Huck Finn told the best—at least I enjoyed them the most. That is a mighty good book, and I should like to hear you read it all. But everything of yours is good for platform reading. You can't go amiss.[33]

Boston was a shrewd choice as site for the first metropolitan performance. Both readers had many friends there, and Pond knew the newspapermen. In Boston Cable was strongly approved as a reconstructed southerner; and his pairing with Twain, now thought of as a citizen of Connecticut, was smiled on as a "literary bridging of the bloody chasm."[34] Beginning on Saturday, November 8, and continuing on November 11, 12, and 13, the *Evening Transcript* carried what became a standard advertisement that strikes the tone which Pond wished to stress throughout the tour. Twain is a comedian; Cable a master of humor and pathos. As in Melrose, Pond presented this first Boston reading as one in a lyceum lecture series, a proceeding he followed elsewhere whenever possible.

> Bay State and Roberts Lyceum Union fifth entertainment. Music Hall, Thursday Evening, Nov. 13, at 8. Mark Twain (Mr. S. L. Clemens), As a Reader of his own superb fun; and Mr. Geo. W. Cable, The distinguished Southern Novelist; presenting the

17

matchless scenes of his own romances. To appear together! Mark Twain's world-famous wit. Mr. Cable's exquisite humor and pathos. A combination of genius and versatility that appeals freshly to the intelligent public. Admission, with reserved seat, 75. Tickets now ready at Music Hall.

The *Transcript,* the *Globe,* the *Journal,* and the *Post* reviewed the performance in their issues for November 14. The *Transcript* did little more than welcome the appearance of Twain but commented more particularly on Cable. The critic observed that Cable's voice had gained in volume since his last appearance but was still better suited to Chickering Hall than to the Music Hall. On the other hand, he was so much improved in "elocution and in dramatic expression" that he managed to give each character a pronounced individuality. He received most applause, however, for "quaint songs peculiar to the creoles of New Orleans." The *Globe* compared Cable to Dickens and praised Twain for his struggle with the German language, his trying conversation with the young lady in the hotel dining room at Lucerne, and his ghost story. The *Journal* noted that all selections were substantially the same as those given on Monday evening in Melrose and reported that the audience filled the hall. The *Post* praised the well-known Twain briefly; then turned to a consideration of Cable:

Mr. Cable is amateurish in his manner, but the dialects of his characters are given well, and all that he says is clear and intelligible. He was received with marked favor, and in response sung a volksong [sic] in a language unfamiliar to the audience, but as he prefaced the singing with a translation of the words, the number was exceedingly pleasing. His tenor voice is sweet and strong, and it is evident that the novelist is a musician also.

All three of these newspapers carried advertisements or announcements on Friday, the fourteenth, for matinee and evening readings in Chickering Hall on the following day. The following week Henry Ward Beecher became the sixth attraction of the lyceum series in the Music Hall, and Miss Kate Field filled Chickering with her three lectures on "The Mormon Monster," "Polygamy in Utah," and "Mormon Treason."

18

Twain was in Providence on Sunday, November 16[35] and in Hartford the following day. Cable presumably had one or two days at home in Simsbury.[36]

The troupe moved next into New York for three performances, one on Tuesday, November 18, and two on the following day. Pond ran the same advertisement that he had given the Boston papers, and the men read to well-filled houses. In the bigger city Twain was not quite so universally known as in Boston, and critics could not take for granted that his name, books, and mannerisms were familiar.

The *Daily Tribune* did not get its report into the issue for November 19, but offered the next day a concise appraisal of the first New York reading. The audience, according to the *Tribune,* consisted principally of ladies; Cable's comic selections roused little more than languid laughter, but "Mary's Night Ride" was liked; and Twain's "A Trying Situation" was specially acceptable. "Mr. Clemens's stories were punctuated with laughter at every few words. Mr. Cable generally received his applause all in a lump at the end."

Long criticisms in the *Times* and in the *Sun* for November 19 were both able but very different in tone and in point of view. The critic for the *Times* was supercilious and cool towards Twain, warm towards Cable, restrained in style. The critic for the *Sun* was indifferent to Cable but liked Twain and made a determined effort to capture some of Twain's spirit by a judicious mixture of description and quotation.

The irony with which the genteel critic for the *Times* considered Twain enters into his first paragraph:

A numerous and enthusiastic audience assembled in Chickering Hall last evening to listen to readings from the writings of Mr. Samuel L. Clemens—who prefers to be known as "Mark Twain"—and Mr. George W. Cable. The gentlemen who read were the gentlemen who had written. The management, in its newspaper advertisements, spoke of the entertainment as a "combination of genius and versatility," but neglected to say which of the gentlemen had the genius and which the versatility. Some of those who were present last evening may have felt justified in coming to the conclusion that Mr. Cable represented both these elements, while Mr. Clemens was simply man, after the fashion of that famous hunting animal one-half of which was pure Irish setter and the other half "just plain dog." Mr. Cable was humorous, pathetic, weird, grotesque, tender, and melodramatic by turns, while Mr. Clemens confined his efforts to the ridicule of such ridiculous matters as aged colored gentlemen, the German language, and himself.

The critic then contrasted the delightful characters created by Cable with such earthy creatures as Huckleberry Finn. When Cable read "A Sound of Drums," this "masterly bit of word-painting was recited with fine elocutionary art, and held the audience spellbound to the close, when a burst of enthusiastic applause recalled Mr. Cable to the stage and compelled him to sing one of the old Confederate war songs that he learned by the camp fire." His reading of "Mary's Night Ride" joined with rare skill "weirdness, tenderness, and melodramatic force."

Twain's "A Trying Situation" is satirized as "one of those peculiar productions which attributes to its author much idiocy, and suggests the thought that it was written in the hope that it would make men deem the writer a very different kind of man." Twain's reading of "A Ghost Story" is handled even more bluntly. The story "had no merit beyond the reader's suggestion that it was a queer story to tell children at bedtime."

The *Sun* printed a critique of nearly one thousand words, most of it about Twain and his performance. Cable was dismissed in a few words: he read with much intensity; an elocutionist would find small praise for his gestures; he frequently used the wrong word by mistake; he sang "Brave Boys Are They" as an encore.

Twain's manner of entering the hall, nearly always impressive to critics, is described in detail:

When Mark Twain walked on the stage, with his chin recently shaved and perceptibly powdered for the occasion, his unruly hair like a halo around his head, and his discouraged expression of countenance, he was welcomed with a prolonged clapping of hands. Without apparently recovering his spirits, he sauntered to the reading desk, felt for it with his right hand, and began.

Twain opened with remarks on his determination to give up lecturing, having bade farewell forever to the platform in the same hall eight or nine years earlier. But lecturers never reform: "There comes in time an overpowering temptation to come out on the platform and give truth and morality one more lift." The reporter noted Twain's habit of looking down sideways into the middle of the desk on which he leaned while his audience laughed. The reader's bored and somewhat lugubrious expression would be only slightly shaken by a twitching under his moustache as he turned his profile to the audience. Then his left hand would seek his pantaloons pocket, he would lean on the reading desk, and proceed in a slow, nasal drawl. For this reporter, Twain's ghost story seems to have been climactic:

> Then he told a ghost story, first advising the nervous people to go home. The story was about a woman with a golden arm who died and was buried, but whose husband concluded afterward to save the arm, and dug it up. In the night of tempest that followed a low steamwhistle whisper chased the man around inquiring: "Who-o-o-o-'s got my go-o-o-olden arm?" He locked himself in his room and went to bed, and the soft steamwhistle whispersighed in his ear: "Who-o-o-o-'s got my go-o-o-olden arm?"
>
> Mr. Twain at this point jumped up two feet in the air and came down with a bang shouting "Nobody!" Everybody else jumped, too.

Both Twain and his official biographer tell a colorful story of an incident during this stay in New York. Twain, as he stepped with his wife out of Chickering Hall into fog and rain following his first night performance, is said to have overheard Richard Watson Gilder talking to an unseen companion about trying to secure and publish Grant's memoirs. Twain had long hoped that Grant would write out his story, and he is supposed immediately to have initiated plans that led to the publication through his own private publishing house of this extremely lucrative work.[37]

During these early days of the tour Twain seems to have thought highly of Cable as a performer. Cable was well pleased with himself all along, although he felt that he somehow struck a new and superior "streak" beginning on November 20, before a small audience at Newburgh, New York.[38] The next night, at Philadelphia, the two authors read in a large hall to a full house, with a number of men standing at the rear. Cable sat on the steps of the "retiring room" and scribbled a happy note to his wife while Mark, on the stage, provoked roars of applause. Going on the stage, Mark had paused long enough to say, "Old boy, you're doing nobly." And it seemed to the elated Cable that he was: even his milder humor had been interrupted with laughter and applause.[39]

The readers gave two performances to huge houses in Brooklyn on Saturday, November 22. Clemens wrote to his wife as he lay in bed the next morning that Henry Ward Beecher and the Dean Sages[40] attended the night show and that Sage came behind the scenes when they finished at ten o'clock.[41] Beecher, who may have taken a professional interest in the techniques of the performers, was a friend and patron of Cable's and a friend of Twain's in addition to being one of Pond's chief lecturing "properties."

On Monday and Tuesday the show moved on to Washington, where it gave two evening performances in the Congregational church. On Tuesday night when Cable walked off after his second number he found three congratulatory visitors in the retiring room—President Chester A. Arthur, a daughter of Frederick T. Frelinghuysen, Arthur's secretary of state, and "another lady," whose name Cable missed. A little later Frederick Douglass came in. This meeting of the President and the famous ex-slave delighted Cable, who wrote ecstatically to his wife: "They met as acquaintances. Think of it! A runaway slave!"[42]

A report on page one of the Washington *Post* for Tuesday, November 25, divides attention very equally between Cable and Twain and prints a pen and ink sketch of each of the readers. Cable is described as having a rich, melodious voice that rose to a high falsetto in its portrayal of female character. His reading of "Mary's Night Ride" seems to have been particularly impressive. Critic and audience "followed Mary and little Alice and the spy in their lonely midnight ride through forest road and across cold streams until they reached the

22

road. How vividly the picture was drawn! and then, when the soldiers sprang up in the road and there was the gleam of carbines and the sound of firing, how one's heart throbbed when the baby cried 'Mother,' and Mary whispered to it and lashed her horse in the same instant, while the spy heightened the dramatic action by his shout of victory."

Time, the critic wrote of Twain, "has no mercy even upon a professional mirth-provoker and has plentifully sifted his hair and heavy drooping moustache with fine white powder":

His face is clean cut as a cameo. He speaks in a sort of mechanical drawl and with a most bored expression of countenance. The aggrieved way in which he gazes with tilted chin over the convulsed faces of his audience, as much as to say, "Why are you laughing?" is irresistible in the extreme. He jerks out a sentence or two and follows it with a silence that is more suggestive than words. His face is immovable while his hearers laugh, and as he waits for the merriment to subside, his right hand plays with his chin and his left finds its way to the pocket of his pants. Occasionally the corners of his mouth twitch with inward fun, but never is a desire to laugh to get the better of him. These characteristics agree so well with his description of himself in his books—Innocence victimized by the world, flesh, and Devil— that one cannot fail to establish the resemblance and laugh at this grotesque image.

The critic also described fully the way in which Twain introduced the "Tragic Tale of a Fishwife":

Twain once went to Germany and wrestled with the language of that country. "There is one disease," he told his audience, "which is sure to affect everybody at some time or other during his life, and that is the disease which prompts a man to learn a foreign language." The audience guessed what was coming and laughed. "I escaped that infection," continued the speaker, in deliberate drollness, "for a long time—the major part of my life, in fact; but I did not escape it entirely. I had learned a smattering of Chinese, one or two Indian dialects and some other kindred classic languages, but nothing serious. The serious part came later. I went to Germany two years ago, with an evil instinct that I could learn the German language. I know better now. [Laughter.] I went to work at it, worked hard and hopefully, fought a good, honest fight with it, but the German language has been in the business longer than I have [laughter] and it came out ahead." Then the audience laughed again, and when

23

the speaker continued to relate his struggles with the nouns and adjectives, and his acquaintance with a dissipated student of Heidelberg, who said he "would rather decline four drinks than one noun," his hearers shook with visible emotion. And this was by way of prelude to the "Tragic Tale of a Fishwife," wherein English words were given the same gender as if they had been German, the result being a comical mixture, absurd to the highest degree.

The critic ended his report by noting that the President would attend the Tuesday performance. On Wednesday the *Post* ran a brief notice headed "The President Enjoys the Fun": "Another large audience greeted Mark Twain and Cable last night. The President was present and seemed to enjoy the entertainment greatly."

On the night of Wednesday, November 26, the "twins of genius" again read in Philadelphia, in Association Hall, and the admiring Cable noted that while Mark recited his "Desperate Encounter with an Interviewer" roars of laughter rolled in as regularly as surf falling on a beach.[43] Cable thought it a great thing to be able to hold his own with "so wonderful a platform figure." This optimistic notion that he held his own with Twain is as far as Cable went in comparing himself with his lecture partner. Repeatedly over the years he expressed vast admiration for Mark, admiration unblurred by vanity and untinctured by envy.

The *Inquirer* for Thursday carried a short report of the performance, devoted almost entirely to Twain, who substituted a new story for one of his usual selections:

One of his yarns contemplated the reform of the human race by preventing the habit of profanity among men. The reform was to be accomplished by substituting mechanical swearing through the means of the phonograph. The effect of this contrivance on shipboard, colored by all the possibilities of swearing in foreign languages, and swearing backwards and multiplying the force of it by placing as many as one hundred and fifty phonographs in different parts of the ship was too much for the most serious audience in the world [sic], and there was a continuous burst of laughter.

Swearing was, of course, one of Twain's accomplishments and delights. As an ex-pilot, ex-miner, and ex-newspaperman he prided himself on the variety and richness of his expletive resources, took a deep interest in swearing as an art, and was ready to acknowledge a master when he heard one. Despite the new yarn and appreciative audience, this same performance in Philadelphia could have been the one that was followed, as Cable remembered it, by Twain's ruefully groaning, "Oh, Cable, I am demeaning myself. I am allowing myself to be a mere buffoon. It's ghastly. I can't endure it any longer."[44] That night and the next day, according to Cable, Twain devoted himself to the study and rehearsal of selections which he deemed justified both as humor and as "literature and art."[45]

Twain and Cable spent Thanksgiving, November 27,[46] with Thomas Nast, cartoonist and lightning artist, and his family in Morristown, New Jersey. During the night Twain prowled about the house and stopped all the clocks to keep them from interfering with his sleep. This is the kind of episode that seems to have established Twain in the mind of Paine and of a good many others as a devastatingly humorous eccentric. Nast gave his impression of the incident in a sketch of his two guests in nightshirts: Twain is gathering clocks of all shapes and sizes, while Cable holds a candle aloft to light the scene. The points of Cable's mandarin-like moustache are represented as coming down to his waist.[47]

The next day the speakers were on the road again. They renewed acquaintances and performed in Baltimore on November 28-29.[48] On December 1 they were in Adams, Massachusetts; and on December 2 they read in Troy, New York, before an "enormous" audience. Here Governor Cleveland is supposed to have heard them. On the morning of the second the traveling companions called on Cleveland in his office at the capitol in Albany. Cable, impressed with the moral strength that he saw in Cleveland's face, came away convinced that the stories of his immoralities were slanders.[49] A comic interlude was furnished by Twain who distinguished himself by sitting casually on buzzers on the desk of the President-Elect and summoning four pages.[50]

The next stops were at Ithaca on December 3 and at Mus-

25

kegon, Michigan, on December 4. While in Muskegon Twain wrote a note of inquiry to Chatto, his English publisher. The readings were going so pleasantly and so profitably that he was eager to know whether he would "draw" if he gave similar readings in the spring or summer in a small hall somewhere in the West End of London. He asserted that he was tempted to try it, because he was having a jolly good time on the platform.[51]

Despite his horror of "taking to the road," Twain did usually enjoy himself when he was actually on the platform before an appreciative audience. Moreover, although he chafed when away from his family, he was chronically restless. Travel, which helped to dispel this restlessness, posed its own special annoyances. Twain particularly disliked the ennui of traveling alone. Pond offered companionship, of a sort; and Cable was expected to supply a more intellectual stimulus. This he did; in addition, he joined Twain in the joyously plaintive singing of Negro spirituals. Unfortunately, he was not in other ways exactly the kind of good company that Twain preferred. He did not drink, he did not tell bawdy stories, he did not play billiards, and he would not travel on Sundays.

Back from Michigan and in New York state again, the men appeared twice in Rochester on Saturday, December 6. Here Cable persuaded Twain to purchase a copy of Malory's *Morte d'Arthur*, an act that had literary repercussions. On Sunday Twain stayed in bed to rest, read, and write.

In Toronto, Canada, on the eighth, Cable wrote to his wife from the big glass "Pavilion" at Horticultural Gardens while Mark "read" to the audience. He and Mark were interrupted, he wrote, by frequent roars of British applause. He remarked (hardly with reference to his own popularity, in view of the ill reputation he had now acquired in his native city) that he had never heard anything like it outside New Orleans. In a few moments, he added, he had to go on to sing two or three Creole songs: "I always shrink from this, the only thing I do shrink from; though it's always encored."[52] Perhaps he felt that there was something unmanly about trilling his Creole songs, or perhaps he could not quite reconcile this part of the program with a devotion to ethics.[53] His critics in New Orleans, particularly his Creole critics, sneered at Cable's singing. Some of them considered this part of his performance undignified to the point of degeneracy, and perhaps Cable knew this. But, as the newspaper reports witness, the songs were extremely popular. H. C. Bunner offered a standard opinion when he described Cable's reading as clever, earnest, and amateurish but added that his singing "caught" everyone. It was artless, but with "go" and lilt and strong, pulsing, wild melodies.[54]

The readers appeared in Toronto under the best possible auspices and were given extraordinary newspaper coverage. On December 6, 8, and 9 advertisements appeared in the *Globe* announcing that the readings would be "Under the Immediate Patronage of His Honour Lieut. Gov. and Mrs. Robinson," and the report after the first performance says that the entertainment was under the auspices of the Ladies' Aid Society of the Metropolitan Church. On December 8 a notice under the heading "Musical and Dramatic" gave the program, observed that the sale of seats had been large, and declared that the fame of Twain, the great humorist, would be sufficient to fill the Pavilion.

On Tuesday, December 9, the *Globe* printed nearly two thousand words on the performance of the previous evening. The reporter described the audience and the introduction "by ex-Aid. Boustead," expressed regret that Twain did not read certain of his best-known stories, paid polite but not enthusiastic attention to Cable, and then settled down to a full report on Twain and his selections. In Twain the reporter apparently felt that he had the real, the American thing, and he tried to preserve for his readers as much as he could of man and words:

He was, of course, received with great applause and for some moments could not proceed. When he did speak it was evident from the first word that the audience would enjoy his reading. After listening to him for five minutes one would be quite ready to accept as solemn truth the story he tells about his prepara-

27

tions for his first lecture, when he found a man who was led to laugh very heartily because of his (Mark's) "drawling infirmity of speech," as he calls it. It is not an infirmity but a peculiarity. His deep voice and his pronunciations of many words are of Missouri, where he was brought up, his nasal twang is of New England where he has spent a good many years, and his drawl is of Mark Twain. Now and again he jerks a short sentence out with wonderful rapidity, but that over, he relapses into his regular gait. He reads, however, with more care than is at first noticeable, and when he is imitating Huck Finn or the old negro telling a ghost story, his utterance changes enough to produce the impression he wishes to produce, but it is always a Huck Finn or a negro who talks like Mark Twain. He is most at home when relating his personal adventures. When he is personating Mark Twain he does it to the life and is an immense success. Every word almost is a joke, every modulation of his voice shows new and unsuspected fun in writings that may have been read over a dozen times. During his readings the house was convulsed with laughter. There were times when all laughed together. There were times when one would see a joke before the others grasped it, and would guffaw aloud, then stop short, till half the crowd laughing at him and the other half at the joke would start off, and the pioneer laugher, reassured, would lead the laugh and keep it up some seconds after the rest were quiet. . . .

The reporter not only took down verbatim a portion of the conversations between Jim and Huck that Twain recited, but he also quoted Twain's introductory remarks:

Ladies and gentlemen,—You find me appointed to read something entitled "King Solermunn," if it may strictly be called reading where you don't use any book, but it is from a book, an unpublished story of mine called "The Adventures of Huckleberry Finn." It is a sort of continuation or sequel, if you please, to a former story of mine, "Tom Sawyer." Huck Finn is an outcast, an uneducated, ragged boy, son of the town drunkard in a Mississippi River village, and he is running away from the brutalities of his father, and with him is a negro man, Jim, who is fleeing from slavery, and these two are in concealment in a wood on an island in the Mississippi River. They can't venture to travel in the daytime, so they hide during the day and travel at night, and they entertain each other with conversations sometimes useful and sometimes otherwise. The story is written from the mouth of Huck Finn.

28

The performers were in Fort Erie, Canada, on December 10,[55] and in Ann Arbor, Michigan, on December 12. They read in Grand Rapids on the night of December 13, after an all-day train trip. The next day, Sunday, Twain probably lay abed writing letters and reading, as usual. Cable, who generally made a round of churches on Sundays, visited a large Baptist church where the preacher recognized him and persuaded him to talk first to the entire Sunday school and then to the infant class. The novelist begged off from addressing the congregation that night. He had begun to feel the stress of travel, for he wrote his wife:

This hasn't been one of my best Sundays. I do not feel that spiritual refreshment I want. But the next one, God willing, will be spent with you in our quiet valley home among our five darlings and our gentle, quiet friends.[56]

Perhaps in his mind he was comparing the "gentle, quiet friends" at home with the sometimes violent friend of his travels.

The troupe was in Toledo on December 15 and in Detroit the next day. The Detroit *Post* made a feature of the visit. In a criticism published on Wednesday, December 16, the reporter described the appearance, dress, and mannerisms of both speakers. Cable's gestures were considered finished to a point of naturalness that forbids the thought of study; his delivery was easy and natural; and his range of voice and manner was remarkable. "Sitting and standing, walking about and gesticulating, he was the character personated." Twain's gait "resembled the motion of a tall boy on short stilts. Infinitely droll looking, he wore a conventional black suit quite out of harmony with his personality."

Like many other critics, the reporter for the *Post* took his color from Twain and attempted to become a wit. Twain had, he wrote, an extraordinary head of stiff hair of no particular color but inclining to a bleached brick-dust shade which had evidently been gone over a few times with a harrow to make the stubborn crop of hirsute delirium tremens stay down for an hour or two. Twain's face was "Yorick come again . . . one of the oddest looking faces ever worn by man." His arms were somewhat short for his length, and unmanageable. His legs were tolerably well under control, but restive; his voice a good strong steady voice in harness until the driver became absent-minded, when it would stop to rest; his neck swan-like and white, but much thicker than a swan's.

In a separate story headed "The Funny Men in Bed," the reporter told of trying to interview Twain the previous afternoon in his room at the Russell House and of being fobbed off with Cable. Twain, in his nightshirt, kept the reporter outside his door. Convinced that anything Twain said was quotable, the reporter put his story in dialogue form:

"Hello. Glad to see you. Can't ask you in, though, as I'm just going to bed."

"I will only detain you a few minutes, Mr. Clemens," apologized the reporter.

"I want to go to sleep. You'd better come around after the lecture. By the way, the *Post* is a good paper. I read an excellent article on copyright the other day which was taken from your paper."

"I would like to ask you a few questions regarding your opinions on copyright privileges," remarked the reporter, who began to imagine that he had gained the humorist's attention at last.

"Ask Mr. Cable. He knows all about copyright. Whatever he says you can put in my mouth and I'll be responsible," replied the literary hero with a tremendous yawn.

"But it won't take you five minutes to answer my questions."

"Too sleepy. I feel the yearning for slumber here," and he tapped his forehead. "If I don't get it now I won't get it at all. Interview Cable in the meantime, and come around and see me after 10 this evening."

The reporter did interview Cable and printed his opinions on copyright, a subject on which Twain seems to have indoctrinated him, in the newspaper for December 18. Twain he returned to at the Russell House billiard room after the evening reading. Twain had just defeated Pond in two games of billiards and "was in high spirits in consequence." The reporter quizzed him in a desultory way on several topics, among them the state of lecturing and of American humor:

"Do you consider the eastern or western states the better field for lecturers and readers?"

"I can't recognize any difference. We have had very large audiences in the eastern cities, and in the West there is no perceptible decrease except when there is a snow storm."

"Is the American taste for humor still growing, in your opinion?"

"Yes, I think so. Humor is always popular, and especially so with Americans. It is born in every American, and he can't help liking it."

"Is it true that the American style of humor is becoming very popular in England?"

"Yes. The liking for American humor over there has become immense. It wakens the people to a new life, and is supplanting the dry wit which formerly passed for humor. American humor wins its own way, and does not need to be cultivated. The English come to like it naturally."

"How about newspaper humorists? Has the American press not become the popular vehicle of humor?"

"It has, undoubtedly. Newspaper paragraphing is comparatively new to us, even, and has met with well-deserved popularity. It is one of the achievements of the age."

On leaving Detroit the two men had about a week of rest and relief from each other's company during the Christmas season, Clemens in Hartford and Cable in Simsbury. This interval at home was not, one judges, a period of total relaxation for Clemens. He was fretting over advance sales for *Huck Finn,* literary pirates, a balky furnace, and a patent clasp supposed to hold babies in their sheets. It was this Christmas, however, that Mark was charmed and soothed by a surprise performance of Livy's dramatization of *The Prince and the Pauper,* played at the home of George Warner. The Clemens girls all took parts: Susy played the Prince; Clara, Lady Jane Grey; Jean, one of Lady Jane's maids. In repetitions, Mark took over the role of Miles Hendon.

The troupe was back on the road in time to appear in Pittsburgh on December 29. To get there, Twain seems to have left Hartford for New York on December 27 and to have traveled all day on Sunday, December 28. Cable must have spoken with very little rest after traveling all day on Monday.[57]

On December 30 the men were in Dayton, Ohio. On the thirty-first they read at Paris, Kentucky, where they spent

31

New Year's day. Twain pridefully wrote his wife of their alert southern audiences:

Whenever we strike a Southern audience they laugh themselves all to pieces. They catch a point before you can get it out & then if you are not a muggins, you *don't* get it out; you leave it unsaid.[58]

On the evening of Friday, January 2, they appeared in Cincinnati at the Odeon, "a beautiful new Hall." On this same day Major Pond departed for New York to supervise other business affairs; and Ozias Pond, the major's brother, joined them. For as long as he was with the tour, Ozias kept a record of events in a notebook of Twain's invention. Twain had presented him with the notebook. "Therefore," Ozias wrote in it, somewhat wryly, "I will make my twenty-fifth attempt to keep a diary."[59]

On January 3 they read again in Cincinnati to crowded houses both matinee and evening. On Sunday, the fourth, in describing examples of Cincinnati's famous Rookwood pottery that he had just seen, Cable reached lyric heights that won Twain's admiration. Twain remarked that his friend could never again describe his emotions as he did in the first flush of enthusiasm. Cable made the effort, however, in a letter to his wife, reserving no superlatives:

Forms of such grace that one delight was to handle them with closed eyes. Colors of such richness, such delicacy, such harmony, such heights & depths as never had I conceived among possibilities. Decorations so original, so life-like, such instantaneous revelations of the errors of our earlier tastes and triumph of truer principles in the covering of surfaces, that one must clasp one's hands and lift & part & drop them and be silent or make little moanings for lack of words. Glazes as soft and warm as a mole's back—no wonder they call it "hair-fur-glaze." And there was one thing more that must be told. A new discovery; a wonderful glaze that has but just been produced and which they are not yet sure of ever producing again. I took a large jar in my arms and held it perpendicularly before my sight: a wild wealth of color, deep, ripe, velvety red struggling with dark sea and orange greens as some alchemist's flame might wrestle in the air with its own rolling smoke. Then I slowly tipped its top toward me, its bottom toward the window's light, and oh! marvellous. Slowly, silently as a panther treads, those wonderful

32

depths of color turned pale and paler—turned from smoke to frost, from frost to tresses of softest hair,—from red and green to purple and grey shot with gleams and floating dots of violets. —Let me stop![60]

Twain had little taste in the arts, other than that of writing, and, except in his rough-riding early work, very properly distrusted his own judgment. Even in literature he had no adequate touchstones to keep him from gross errors in evaluating the sentimental, the pseudo-comic, the faulty in tone, or the grotesquely overplotted, whether in his own work or in that of others. Cable's outburst may well have been the kind of thing that made Twain consider his companion a great intellectual.

Mark and Ozias went out to see the potteries on Sunday. Mark was charmed. He presented a tea caddy to Ozias and made "quite an investment" in pottery for himself. On Saturday, the preceding day, he had been to a phrenologist to have his head analyzed; and Ozias, infected with the humor of the two writers and amazed at Twain's extravagance, punned feebly: "There was nothing in it."

If captivated by Cable's taste and eloquence while in Cincinnati, Twain was also intensely irritated by his parsimony. During the early days of the tour he had grumbled very little about Cable, but after a few weeks his complaints were frequent. Now, using the initial "K" to represent "Cable," as he sometimes did when he was both cautious and mordant, Twain confided in Livy that Cable had just piled out a whole trunk of washing, "all saved up since we were on the road last." Considering this an imposition Twain called it to the attention of Ozias, who declared that he would make Cable pay for the wash. Irritated though he was, Twain retained some sense of proportion and admitted to Livy that he liked "K" better and better, but that his "closeness" was a queer streak.[61] Probably Ozias wrote to his brother about Cable's expenses, for Cable and Pond seem to have had a vexed exchange of letters. The major poured oil on the waters, writing on January 22 from New York a letter which Cable must have received in Minneapolis:

33

My dearly beloved.

Your letter is received. If it gave you pain it ought to make you feel better after the pain. What good is a friend if one can't abuse him? I had a good many things on my mind & was at that time disappointed. If you had the bills to pay you would see, & at times I am cross. I did not mean to be. You may abuse me all you like & I will love you still. I am sorry Mark *will not* keep on through March & April.[62] It would pay you much better than anything you could do. It is dull & I have changed all my calculations & return you to where I can see you. . . .[63]

Pond, it appears, had been caught between the upper and the nether millstones.

The touring trio caught the 8:15 train from Cincinnati for Louisville on the morning of the fifth, and Mark was interviewed immediately upon their arrival at the Galt House. Next came a reception at the Press Club at 4:30, followed by a visit to the Pendennis Club and a performance at Liederkranz Hall. Ozias noted in his diary that after the reading "Marse" Henry Watterson "invited us all to the Pendennis Club to lunch." (Perhaps Ozias meant to a late supper.) "I modestly declined, but the others take everything they can get." The next night after another appearance Mark and Cable went again to the Pendennis Club for supper. Considering the kind of refreshments for which the hospitable Pendennis Club is famous, the education of George W. Cable doubtless proceeded apace.

The tour enjoyed a good press in Louisville. "Marse" Henry was distantly related to Clemens through the Lamptons—that is, on Clemens' mother's side; and on January 4 the *Courier-Journal,* Watterson's influential paper, prepared the way for the speakers with an editorial announcing appearances for Monday and Tuesday evenings and quoting approximately three hundred words of praise from the *Daily Evening Traveler* (Boston). Watterson, like most other critics, had not yet discovered that Clemens was a great novelist. He identified him as "the most popular humorous writer in the English language," and called Cable "the distinguished Southern novelist." He noted that Cable had given delightful readings

34

in Louisville the preceding season, proved to be as "gifted a reader" as a writer, and "made a host of friends" in the city. This same issue of the *Courier-Journal* carried a separate announcement and an advertisement with an accompanying photograph. The paper for January 5 repeated the announcement and ran a short article that included the program for the first performance.

On January 6 the *Courier-Journal* reviewed the performance of the preceding evening, noticing at the same time the major competing attractions. "Pretty little Minnie Palmer" acted, sang, and danced in a light love story at Macauley's Theater; Mlle. Aimee charmed, too, with songs and dances in *Mam'zelle* at the Masonic Temple Theater; a good company presented *A Hoop of Gold* — a thrilling melodrama — at the Grand Theater; and *Peck's Bad Boy* amused a large audience at Harris's Museum.

Despite competition and rain, Twain and Cable had a good house. Cable's selections were said to be familiar from his earlier appearance but had "lost none of their charm," particularly his pathetic and moving story of "Mary's Night Ride." Twain's humor was said to be indescribable and inimitable; and his "Tragic Tale of a Fishwife" was greeted with continuous laughter.

The program for January 6 followed this critique, and this second reading was noticed briefly on January 7. This time Twain's "Why I Lost the Editorship" and Cable's repeated account of Mary's ride were favorites of an evening that was "in every way delightful."

In Indianapolis on Wednesday, January 7, Ozias made Mark happy by playing billiards with him and Cable was made happy, no doubt, by testimony on the front page of the Indianapolis *Journal* to his growing reputation as a champion of civil rights for the Negro. The January *Century* printed "The Freedman's Case in Equity," Cable's most important statement on the Negro question, and public reaction was immediate and violent. The story in the *Journal*, a "Washington Special," was headed "Southern Appreciation of Mr. Cable":

Two Southern Democrats at the capital yesterday were discussing current literary topics, when one of them suddenly asked: "Have you read Gable's article in the Century?"

"No," replied the other. "What is the article about, and who the blank is Gable?"

"Oh," said the first Democrat savagely, "it is an article in favor of the 'nigger,' and full of abuse and lies about the Southern people. Haven't you heard of Gable? George W. Gable is his name. He is that New Orleans man who writes books and goes around the country reading them in public. He brags that his grandfather and father were both slaveholders, and then says that it was not their fault, that they did not know any better. The article would be bad enough if it had been written by a Northern man; coming from a Southern man it is an insult."

"Well, I do not want to read it. I should think Gable would emigrate to the North and stay there. We have no use for such men in the South."

It is evident that these indignant Southerners do not appreciate Mr. Cable's literary efforts.

Perhaps because of interest aroused by this story out of Washington, the Plymouth Church was filled to overflowing that night, and many were turned away. The report in the *News* on the next day was very brief, but the critic for the *Journal* was enthusiastic. This was, he wrote, the "most unique and thoroughly enjoyable entertainment ever given in Indianapolis." Cable read substantially the same selections he read in Indianapolis the previous winter, but he had them "in much better control," for earlier he had stayed too close to the printed page. Mark Twain was "simply indescribable" in his readings from *Huck Finn*, his talk on the German language, his whistling story, and the "trying situation" in which he talked over old times with a young woman at Lucerne. Twain's last number, his story of the golden arm, raised the audience from its seats promptly at quarter past ten o'clock.

At seven o'clock on the morning of the eighth, the travelers rose to prepare for a nine-hour journey to Springfield, Illinois. En route to Springfield Mark spent an hour rewriting a boasting match (probably from Chapter 3 of *Life on the Mississippi*) so that he and Cable could hurl brags at each other "for Pond's amusement" at night in their rooms.[64]

The Springfield paper gave adequate but not extensive notice to the performers. On January 7 the *Illinois State Register* quoted approximately 150 words about them from the Boston *Post* (for November 14) and the *Illinois State Journal* evened the score with a comparable extract from the Boston *Globe*. On the eighth the *Register* and the *Journal* published brief criticisms. According to the *Register*, one of the largest and most cultivated audiences of the season filled Chatterton's Opera House; the *Journal* thought it "safe to say that few audiences have congregated there composed of more intelligent and cultivated people."

The troupe left Springfield for St. Louis on the morning of the ninth at 6:35, "much to the disgust of Mark," who despised early rising. An accident delayed their arrival in St. Louis and gave them an exciting ten minutes. Ozias wrote in his diary that the engine and baggage car jumped the track just as their train was moving onto the bridge over the Mississippi. The wrenched cars crashed together, and the passengers, except for Cable and Ozias, rushed for the doors. Twain, the old river pilot, ran with the others but made a joke of it later, saying that he had known he would be all right if he got into the river. The three entertainers walked across the bridge, took a car to the Southern Hotel, and that night were welcomed by a large audience "in the old Library Hall."

Cable probably found a letter dated January 7 from J. B. Pond waiting for him in St. Louis. The major, still hopeful, advised Cable to continue the tour through March if Twain could be persuaded. He "did so hate" to leave the tour, would try to visit them soon, and transmitted Henry Ward Beecher's love to both.

The next day, Saturday, January 10, they played to matinee and night audiences, both good, although the night crowd was not unusually so, because Saturday night was not popular in St. Louis "with the better element," according to Ozias.

On Sunday Cable visited the churches, and Mark spent the day in bed reading the manuscript of a story submitted to him for his opinion "by a young lady." Twain thought the story was "of no account, like all the other stories that had been submitted to him to read." That night Ozias ordered supper in his room, and he and Mark had "a jolly feast" together, as they frequently did. On this particular night Mark held Ozias enthralled with the story of the mutineers of the *Bounty* and of their settling on Pitcairn Island. It was a new story to Ozias and "a wonderfully romantic reality." "The great Humorist" always held his attention, Ozias declared, and on this night more than ever.

Sometime during this stay in St. Louis, James Lampton, the original for Colonel Sellers in *The Gilded Age,* called on Clemens. When he appeared, Clemens set ajar the door to Cable's adjoining room and let the "golden dream-talk" float in. After Cousin Jim had accepted free tickets for the reading and had bowed himself out, Cable stuck his head in at the door. "That was Colonel Sellers," he said.[65]

The newspapers in St. Louis, which considered itself Sam Clemens' home metropolis, gave the visiting readers numerous and excellent notices. On Sunday, January 4, five days before the first reading, the *Missouri Republican* carried a brief advance notice in the column headed "Amusements."[66] An announcement on January 5 gave the place (Mercantile Library Hall) and the dates for the three proposed performances. A third notice, on January 7, announced the opening of the sale of reserved seats, and a fourth, on January 8, declared that prospects for audiences were "fine."

Advance publicity came to a climax on Friday, January 9. Both the *Republican* and the *Globe-Democrat* carried double-column front-page cuts of the two speakers, and the *Post-Dispatch* carried a long interview. In this story Clemens and the reporter combined to squeeze humor from the near-accident on the railway bridge:

"We had," he [Clemens] said, "just reached that portion of the bridge which overhangs the crystal waters of the Mississippi River when a misunderstanding arose between the forward and rear portions of the train. The engine conceived the intention of leaving the track upon which the rest of the train was and moving upon another one, while the remainder of the train decided to remain where it was. The result was that one of the forward passenger cars was switched diagonally across the track. If we had not been going very slowly at the time the whole train would have left the track."

"Personally, I suppose, you had no fears, being familiar with the river currents?"

"Not in the slightest. It would not have discommoded me in the least to have been tossed in the Mississippi. I know the river thoroughly. It was the other people I was thinking of."

"I noticed that you seemed very anxious about the other people," Mr. Cable remarked with a quiet smile.

"It's no wonder," Mr. Clemens resumed. "There was a continuous kind of jolting which became more and more ominous and suggestive as the train advanced. A sense of crumbling— something crumbling underneath beneath us, where stability was of the highest importance to us all personally, became very prominent. I fully expected the bridge to break down—I always have done so when I crossed it—and my anxiety for the safety of the other passengers led me to leap quite hastily for [sic] my seat and make a rush for the nearest exit. I wanted to get out and see what was the matter so that I could intelligently supply the required relief."

"And you got these [sic]?" the reporter asked.

"Yes, but unfortunately, too late to be of any service. The train had stopped of its own accord. There were not many people hurt in the accident."

"How were they injured?"

"They happened to be in front when I was going out. . . ."

On Saturday the *Post-Dispatch* carried a review of the first reading, and a reminiscent anecdote which illustrates a rather common attitude taken towards Clemens' financial successes. His contemporaries do not seem to have resented his prosperity, but they liked to remember his straitened beginnings:

I wonder if Mark Twain, in his prosperity and fame, when he can fill a hall on short notice, remembers the first lecture he delivered in St. Louis. It was a good many years ago, before Twain had made a national reputation. He was in St. Louis, having just come from California, and was scarcely known to any one. One day a young business man, who was running a mission school in the northern part of the city, announced to his friends that he was going to have a good lecture at his school.

They asked who was going to lecture and he said Mark Twain. This was Hebrew to most of them. Twain had a lot of his usual style of posters printed, announcing the lecture and stating that a lot of prizes would be given, among which were ten smooth auger holes and others of a similar funny kind. The evening came and went and the young man's friends asked him how the lecture came off. "Oh, not very well," said he, "we had bad weather and the people somehow wouldn't come."

"How much did you take in, anyhow?"

"Only $8," was the mournful reply. Eight dollars was a bigger sum to the lecturer then than $800 is now.

The *Republican* gave Twain and Cable notices in three places in its Saturday issue. The "Local and Suburban" column reported that the visitors were greeted by a large audience at Mercantile Library Hall; the "Local Personals" named Clemens and Cable at the head of the list of "principal arrivals" at the Southern Hotel; and a critic devoted approximately seven hundred words to their reading of Friday night. The critic considered Cable's tenor voice much too light for a large hall, but reported that he aroused considerable enthusiasm with some of his readings and with his Creole songs. Clemens fascinated and convulsed his audience with his German language sketch, the "Tragic Tale of the Fishwife," "A Trying Situation," readings from *Huck Finn,* and a ghost story about the old man who stole the coppers from a dead woman's eyelids.

The *Globe-Democrat* and the *Republican* both gave space to the visitors in their Sunday issues. The reporter for the *Globe-Democrat* attempted an appraisal, "literary" in tone, of the personalities, manners, and abilities of the performers. Neither, the reporter thought, could take a prize in an oratorical contest. Their gestures were awkward, and they spoke haltingly; yet in Twain the awkward manner seemed "to be quite the right thing." Cable's Creole songs were very effective, making perhaps the most distinct and lasting impression of the whole entertainment.

The *Republican,* in one of its stories, reviewed the final reading under the heading: "Twain-Cable. The Twain Say Farewell, Though a Cable Binds Them to St. Louis Hearts."

At this third reading Twain told his Jumping Frog story and, for an encore, "how the man in Missouri was cured of stammering by whistling whenever he found he could not find his words." The critic considered the readings worthwhile if only to introduce Cable's Creole songs to the country.

The Sunday *Republican,* moved perhaps by the storm that had just burst over the publication of "The Freedman's Case in Equity," printed a long, interesting interview with Cable devoted to the meaning of the word "Creole," the death of John Richling (in the novel *Dr. Sevier)*, the evils of the Louisiana parish prisons, and the folklore of Louisiana Negroes. Because of the Creoles' dislike for Cable and the heated discussion that was taking place regarding his treatment of them in fiction and in historical essays,[67] the early part of this interview would have had keen interest for St. Louisans. In this interview Cable distinguished between Creoles and Acadians, as he did in his writings, and stressed the proud status of the Creoles. The word "Creole" carries with it, he said, a qualification of peculiar excellence derived from the original root of the word, which signifies "cultivated."[68] The Acadians of Louisiana were, unlike the Creoles, the "poor white trash" of the old regime, but they had already begun to assume positions of dignity, Cable declared, while they retained much of the beauty and simplicity of their former status. As for Richling, whose death was regretted by many readers, Cable asked, "What else could I have done?" and added that the book "required his death to make the character complete." Discussing the folklore of the Negroes of Louisiana, Cable referred to his article on the subject already prepared (perhaps "Creole Slave Dances," which appeared in the *Century* for February, 1886, or "Creole Slave Songs," in the April issue). The harsh treatment of slaves in Louisiana "put a strange melancholy tone into their folklore, and the superstitions, legends, songs, and pictures are most pathetically weird."

Cable and Ozias stood waiting with bated breath in the Southern Hotel on Monday morning, January 12, while Mark, enraged by the necessity for rising in time to catch a

41

train at 9:40, attacked a refractory window shutter. Ozias noted in his diary that Mark won this bout.

The party arrived in Quincy, Illinois, that afternoon. Here Clemens and Cable stayed with Sam's relatives by marriage, the widow of Erasmus Mason Moffett, and her daughters. The two men had their photograph taken with the Moffetts,[69] and that night they read to an audience that packed the Opera House to its doors.

Like most of the river towns, Quincy (named after John Quincy Adams), thought of Twain as belonging to the region; however, the *Daily Journal* for Saturday, January 10, announced the coming reading in terms which though friendly hardly showed close familiarity with Twain's history:

Mr. Samuel L. Clemens—Mark Twain—is a Western man. We understand that he used to be a pilot on the Mississippi river. At all events, he once lived in Hannibal, and at another time in Keokuk. We hope to see our citizens give Mr. Clemens a royal welcome. We know that he and Mr. Cable will entertain the audience that greets them royally.

But the entertainment was not as royal as anticipated. The critic writing in the paper for January 13 was unrelievedly disappointed in the performance of Cable and not much better pleased by Twain. Apparently Quincy disapproved of the genteel tradition as exemplified by Cable, preferring a robuster kind of literature and entertainment. Twain was preferred in print to in person.

A very large and fashionable audience (drawn thither by the celebrity of Mr. Clemens) greeted "Mark Twain" and Mr. Cable at the opera house last night, and were fairly well entertained.

Mr. Cable is a small, weak, affected, effeminate-looking man, with a womanish voice. He is affected in dress and affected in voice. He seems to be trying to imitate Mark Twain, in the matter of a limping, halting, hesitating speech. The fact is that Mark Twain has enough of this unvaluable eccentricity to answer all the purposes of this combination.

Mr. Cable's first recitation was tiresome. It was nothing, very long drawn out. It was all about a creole Frenchman borrowing a dollar of an acquaintance.

42

His second recitation was a little better. He represented the Irish woman in a fairly "amateurish" way. But there was not much to it.

In his third appearance he sang some African Creole refrains fairly well, as we think. This was the best number in the programme.

He recited Mary Richling's ride at his fourth appearance. This was a serious recitation, and was given about the average schoolboy fashion. Mr. Cable is no doubt an elegant and capable writer, but as a reader he is sadly lacking in cultivation. There is nothing fine, or finished, or artistic about his readings. Of course he knows this, probably, better than anyone else. We mean such fineness and such finish as was found in Forrest and Adams, and as we find in Booth, and McCullough, and Barrett, and Mayo, and Keane.

If Mr. Cable should attempt to make a tour of this country alone,—the third night would just about end him. Mark Twain can hold him up for a long time, for Mark Twain is quite another sort of a man. Mark Twain is a sizeable, substantial, sensible, manly-looking and manly-spoken fellow; a man cut out after the pattern of a man, and with the speech and action of a man; a capable, brainy-looking fellow.

There is no discount in Twain's wit. It is there; and it is genuine wit; and reader, let me tell you something! It is much better in his books than it is on the stage—much better. It is condensed in his books. On the stage it is too long, too long drawn out. Twain is too long in coming to a point, and he dwells on it too long, after he does get to it. Wit and humor are a something that surprises the mind. If the "point" of a joke can be anticipated, the life is taken from the joke. It is the pleasant surprise on a point that should be quickly touched and quickly passed. He takes the charm and the sparkle from his funny point by hanging it too long.

Twain's first recitation was his best—by all means. In that he didn't dwell. He drove straight ahead to the end of it. It was a pleasant recitation. Twain's stories are funny, and he tells them in a droll way.

To our notion, the biggest part of the show was Mark Twain himself. And when a man says "I saw Mark Twain last night," he has said the largest thing that can be said about the whole affair. Mark Twain is a famous character—and there is something in human nature that makes us wish to see famous characters. We cannot conscientiously set a very high estimate upon the Twain-Cable entertainment. To see Mark Twain is an event in itself; but no one would particularly care to hear the Twain-Cable entertainment repeated. Little, plain, simple, unpretend-

43

ing Bob Burdette[70] gave an entertainment at our opera house one night, all by himself, that discounted the Twain-Cable entertainment a thousand per cent. Bob's lecture was rich in wit and humor, and rich in pathos. It was a feast of rich things.

We congratulate Dr. Marks upon the large attendance last night. An audience like that adds to his wealth and cheers his spirits.

In Hannibal on Tuesday, the thirteenth, Twain and Cable stayed with friends. Pond "made out," though badly, at the Park Hotel. A flood of reminiscences was set off among the residents by Sam Clemens' return to his old home, and a sizable crowd attended the reading, though not as large, Ozias noted cynically, as in other places. Clemens was, of course, in great demand among old friends.

On Wednesday they arrived late in Keokuk, Iowa, delayed by a storm. Clemens had an emotional reunion with his three pensioners: his mother, his brother Orion, and Orion's wife, Mollie. Jane Clemens, Sam's mother, had left Fredonia, New York, to live with Orion in Keokuk about two years earlier. When she left New York Sam simply added twenty-five dollars each month to the sum that he was already sending the visionary Orion and his wife.

The day was a great one for the Clemenses. Jane Clemens attended the reading at the Keokuk Opera House, and that night, when asked if she could still dance, rose "and at eighty-one tripped as lightly as a girl."[71] The visit was tremendously stimulating for Mark. Late that night he wrote to Livy that he had been meeting "slathers" of ancient friends and having worlds of talk for three days—no chance to sit down and write, "I love you, sweetheart!" "Infinite great deeps of pathos" had rolled their tides over him, but he had just had a beautiful evening with "Ma," who was her old beautiful self—a nature of pure gold. It was too bad that her talents had gone to waste. What books she could have written![72] Apparently still bathed in happy memories of his boyhood and of his visit with Ma, Mark wrote to Orion from Chicago on Friday morning that he had enjoyed a *perfect* twenty-four hours in Keokuk, with the sort of social activity that produces rest instead of fatigue.[73]

44

The Keokuk newspaper, the *Daily Gate City,* showed satisfactory awareness of the importance of this visit by the great
former citizen and was more than adequate in the coverage
it gave the entertainment. On January 8 the approaching
visitation was announced with unusual magniloquence:

Mr. Samuel L. Clemens—"Mark Twain"—and Mr. George W.
Cable, will give a reading at the Keokuk opera house on the evening of the 14th inst. This is in large part a personal visit on
the part of Mr. Twain. He once lived in Keokuk and in Hannibal and so he gives readings in those places only, on his way
from St. Louis to Chicago. His mother and brother live in
Keokuk. He reads in Chicago the evening following his appearance here. Nothing gives distinction to a place like great and
famous persons. A part of their distinction all their fellow-citizens
share. In the thirty years since he left Keokuk Mr. Clemens has
made himself one of the famous men of his time. He is today
the American author whose writings have the largest circulation
and yield the most profit. . . . His work as a writer has made its
own way and he is the only American author who can make a
hundred thousand dollars a year by his literary work. He is the
foremost living humorous writer in the world and Cervantes
and but one or two others have ever lived who were greater as
creators of humor than he. It will probably be the last time that
Mr. Twain will ever visit Keokuk and he and Mr. Cable will no
doubt be met by a great audience and a generous welcome. We
presume that there will be many in neighboring towns and on
farms hereabouts who will want to see and hear these two emi-
nent authors.

On January 14 the *Gate City* expressed renewed local pride
and interest in Twain and declared that Cable was the first
southern novelist to take his place among the immortals. The
performance on the night of the fourteenth was reviewed in
the paper for the fifteenth. The audience was fully repaid,
the critic felt, for fighting the fiercest storm of the season:
Cable was clever, Twain convulsing. Cable's Creole songs and
his "Mary's Night Ride" were well received. Twain re-
sponded to encores with his stuttering story and a sailor yarn
and closed the entertainment by detailing his experience with
the duello in his days of roughing it in the rowdy west.

In the newspaper for January 14 a critic attempted to
weigh Cable and to place him in his proper literary pigeon-

45

hole. The critic begins by depreciating his own familiarity with Cable's work:

> It is not only young critics like Mr. Arthur Pendennis who look through volumes, meditate an opinion over their cigar, and have a shrewd trick of gathering in a very few moments such a dazzling richness of information upon subjects they want to be critics about as will astonish their mammas at home as well as themselves three months later.

He confesses that he has read only *Dr. Sevier,* "Madame Delphine," and "those New Orleans stories" by which Cable became first known. He likes the short stories better than the novel, because "as Browning phrases it, in the first his power exceeds and in the latter 'comes short in.'" Cable is said to have done excellent work but not, as yet, his best. "There has been no better writing in American literature than his. And yet so far he has only written fragments and you long for his completed work. . . . He is plowing a head-furrow in many fields and he scarce knows yet what furrow steadily to go on in."

Pond and Cable left Keokuk early for Burlington, Iowa, their next stop, but Twain stayed over until the last minute in order to see more of his mother. (In December Twain had made Pond rearrange the tour, cutting out one day in Chicago in order to leave more time for Keokuk.)[74] Now bad weather delayed his arrival at Burlington, and by the time he reached the platform Cable had been holding the small audience for more than an hour and a half. Mark cut himself shorter than he wanted to and didn't talk well, because he felt himself "handicapped by the hellish circumstances."[75]

The Burlington newspapers — the *Daily Hawkeye* and the *Daily Gazette* — welcomed the visit of the novelists favorably and copiously. For once Twain was accepted as a literary man, not just a humorist. The *Gazette* for January 15 carried a box advertisement to announce their advent and the *Hawkeye* assessed their merits in an article:

> . . . Mark Twain is well known for many years as occupying a high position in American literature, and stands perhaps without a rival in the domain of American humor. He has made millions

46

laugh by his books and entertained many a refined audience from the platform. He will do so to-night. Mr. Cable is a new man on the platform to the public, and comparatively so also in literature, being a young man. He is already standing by the force of his genius and persevering industry in the front rank of American authors. He has risen rapidly into literary fame, and to-day he ranks as the finest and most thorough delineator of character in our literature.

On the sixteenth both the *Hawkeye* and the *Gazette* printed reports of the reading on the night of the fifteenth. They lamented the storm that kept listeners away and delayed the arrival of Twain and found the contrast between Cable and Twain was all that Major Pond had hoped for. The *Hawkeye* thought Cable delicate and graceful, Twain large, awkward, and "inclined to be uncouth." Twain began his part of the entertainment by explaining his delay. The train, an hour late in leaving Keokuk, broke something on the way. It took forty-five minutes to decide the dispute over what was broken (a cam rod, a ram rod, or a lightning rod, according to the *Gazette)* and five minutes to repair the damage. The *Gazette* particularized on the success of Cable in holding the audience with his readings and songs and regretted that the lateness of the hour kept Twain from adding readings from *Huck Finn* to those he gave from earlier books. The *Hawkeye* for Saturday morning continued its praise of Twain and Cable with notes in the column headed "City Briefs." Cable's Narcisse "as presented by him on the platform" is called "a gem with a golden setting."

From Friday, January 16, through Monday the touring group made headquarters in Chicago, reading there once on Friday, twice on Saturday, and in Evanston on Monday. Ozias noted on Friday that they had a very good audience and on Saturday that their two large audiences showed great enthusiasm. Twain, in a long letter to Livy begun on Saturday night and finished on Sunday afternoon, said that they had three "big" audiences in the "noble" Central Music Hall, despite a fearful storm. Saturday night, he thought, marked his greatest personal triumph. He played his "new bill," with the story of the Jumping Frog told in the quickest time on record (thirteen minutes), the description of the way Tom and Huck set Jim free (twenty-five minutes), and the yarn about Governor Gardiner (ten minutes). Nothing, he told Livy, could beat that jumping frog story when one is feeling good and has the right audience. Moreover, his new plan enabled him to subordinate Cable. The new plan called for Cable's opening the show with a fifteen-minute talk while the house assembled; and even with all the encores the two of them did not hold the audience for more than two hours. Sam confided joyfully to Livy that now "only half the house hears C's first piece — so there isn't too much of C. any more — whereas heretofore there has been a thundering sight too much of him."[76]

The readings in Chicago were well advertised. The *Tribune* carried notices on January 12 through 17 and in the issue for Saturday, January 17, praised the two readers about equally. The reporter estimated at eight hundred the crowd that braved the storm on Friday night to attend the performance. In his opinion, the contrast between the two men brought out the merits of each in strong relief. Twain's dry, drawling fun was irresistible and kept his audience in a perpetual roar, but Cable's humor was of deeper quality.

"Mary's Night Ride" was a "poem in prose." Twain unwittingly created a great deal of merriment by failing to find the proper exit leading to the waiting-room, where he sat during his associate's recitations. He crossed the stage twice, tried every door, and was amazed at the great number of wrong doors he could find. He appeared to be as greatly amused as the laughing lookers-on, and finally dove through a doorway after murmuring, "Guess I rehearsed with the wrong door." "I admire this elegant building," said Mr. Cable, laughing heartily at the other's discomfiture, "but I do think a guide should be provided for strangers."

A large audience turned out in Evanston despite intense cold. The reporter for the Evanston *Index* of January 24 wrote that the audience "listened with interest to George W. Cable" and "roared with laughter at every appearance of Mark Twain." Cable read only from *Dr. Sevier*, which was a disappointment, as he was considered to be "associated in the general mind with his Creole sketches and dialect;" however, his Creole songs were "a pleasing deviation from the program." Twain ended his story of the golden arm by shouting *"You* have" so loud as to bring the audience to their feet, "and before they could reseat themselves he had bowed 'good night' and left the stage."

Back in Chicago after this reading, Ozias and the performers had a cozy supper in Mark's room. The next three days they made one-night stands in Wisconsin at Janesville, Madison, and LaCrosse, playing to a packed house at Madison in the Methodist church and to another at LaCrosse. At LaCrosse Mark indulged himself in some pie crust at the depot that, to the regret of his companions, made him "a little sharp."

On Friday and Saturday, January 23 and 24, they read in St. Paul and Minneapolis, having large crowds for both matinee and evening readings in Minneapolis. The *Daily Globe* (St. Paul) for January 24 reported that approximately one thousand attended the Friday reading in the Market Hall: "Twain supplied the greatest amount of humor, though Cable developed the most versatility."[77] The two men introduced themselves, Cable opening the show by explaining that he was not Mark Twain. On the morning of the twenty-fourth they moved their headquarters to the West Hotel in Minneapolis and were immediately interviewed by a reporter from the *Tribune.* The interview and a review of the performance totaled a column and a half in the newspaper the following day. The reporter described each performer in detail. Twain, now quite grey, came on the stage with a comical, shuffling, sidewise gait. His gestures were eloquent. Cable had a very long brown moustache and beard, a prominent forehead, small, bright eyes, small features, and a light, quick voice. Everything about him indicated a nervous, sensitive, imaginative temperament. The interview contained Twain's stock remarks for reporters: he had hoped to set out with a "menagerie" of performers; he wanted someone to keep him in countenance on the stage and to help him impose on the audience; he wanted good company on the roads and at the hotels. "A man can start out alone and rob the public, but it's dreary work, and it's a cold blooded thing to do."

49

At the afternoon performance in Minneapolis as the last item on the program, Twain told a variant on his story of the golden arm. This time it was a tale of an old woman who died and of an old man who got up during the night and stole the coppers from her eyelids. The ghost of the old woman returned, wailing, "Who's got my money? I want my money." As the story went on, the wind rose, and the moaning of the wind and the wailing of the ghost alternated until the audience was keyed to a high pitch. Twain moved towards the footlights as he wailed and moaned, gradually crouching, hands outstretched, the tension of the audience increasing as his fingers hooked themselves into claws. Then there was a crash as he stamped both feet, threw up his hands, and yelled "Boo!" The effect was satisfactorily tremendous.

On the night of Monday, January 26, the readers appeared in the Philharmonic Hall in Winona, Minnesota, and then turned back to Madison, Wisconsin.[78] Here they played again in the basement of the Methodist church to an appreciative audience. Next day—January 28—the reporter for the *Wisconsin State Journal* contrasted the appearance of Cable with that of Twain, describing Cable as an unusually small man, symmetrically proportioned, weighing perhaps ninety-five pounds:

He is erect, bears himself handsomely and gracefully, and is the embodiment of refinement and culture. His complexion is dark, and harmonizes with his hair. A full beard adorns his face, and his mustaches [*sic*] are long and twisted into a suggestion of his name. His features are delicately moulded, and his brow is broad and full, and indicative of the intellectuality of its possessor. Mr. Cable has a voice which though of a tenor turn, possesses a nasal twang.

The picture presented of Twain conforms to lines usually emphasized: he is active, strong, masculine of feature, his nose is full and straight, his somewhat sunken eyes always on the alert, his hair and moustache tinged with grey.

This same issue of the *Wisconsin State Journal* printed a letter to Cable from a Negro correspondent living in Madison and an answer written by Cable on the day of publication. Arthur B. Lee, the Negro, thanked Cable for the hope raised by his article, "The Freedman's Case in Equity." Cable replied in terms which stress his interest in the Negro and at the same time reveal his characteristically non-aggressive, gradualist approach to race problems:

I thank you most heartily for your letter of 21st inst., received only last night. It is a comfort and a reward to me. I am proud and grateful to say that I have many such from colored men, and also from white men, both north and south.

I am tempted to take the liberty of saying that men of color who can write such letters as these, ought to write to and for the public, and especially to add that in my belief nothing will work more powerfully for the *special* interests of the colored people than for such men to make themselves felt in terse, brief, pointed utterances upon current topics of *general* public interest,—upon interests common to all. This will be to utilize that "touch of nature" that "makes the whole world akin."

When colored men get to writing for white men's newspapers from the standpoint of common citizenship and mutual interests, then we shall see not one or two or half a dozen white men writing in behalf of freedmen's rights, but whole communities yielding those rights.

In short, let all colored men patiently, persistently and with all possible intellectual skill ignore their African origin and do, say and seek everything purely, only and entirely as American citizens, equally interested with all other American citizens in *all* the rights of *all*. I do not, by any means, imply that the part of wisdom is to let the greater—at least the larger—include the less. Let colored men show such sagacious, active interest in the rights and interests of all men, that all men, shall gradually be won to regard them as valuable accessions to the community, and most valuable when most free.

Pardon me if my deep interest in the advancement of colored men has led me to speak too freely. . . .

From Madison the troupe moved to Milwaukee. Here a reporter for the *Sentinel* interviewed Cable and wrote a story that appeared in his paper on January 30. In the interview Cable declared, as he did on other occasions, that the main characters in *Dr. Sevier* were modeled on life and the main incidents were true ones. The Richlings, he said, were married in Milwaukee, and "somewhere up here is this little

51

woman and her daughter, if they are not dead." When asked why a chorus of southern newspapers had recently attacked him, Cable replied that the hostility dated back to the period when he depicted the hard lives of the quadroons "in old times" and that the opposition had developed as he continued to champion the rights of the black man.

Ozias seems to have had a heart attack at Madison; nevertheless he accompanied the tour to Milwaukee, where he took to his bed. At this point a tug of war began between Clemens and J. B. Pond. The major wished to remain snugly ensconced at the Everett House in New York, but like most men, he lacked the force of character necessary to hold out against Clemens. He wrote sadly to Cable on January 30, attempting to enlist his aid and sympathy:

My dear, dear friend:

Your kind favor of the 26th with Dr. Trehune's enclosure, I have written the Dr. & offered a date for $100 also the same to my friend Wm. Cloflin. I certainly shall try to place all the time in March & April that I can.

Your letter from Madison & the sad news about Ozias has completely upset me. I feared the cold weather too much for him. Poor boy. I can never thank you & Mark or repay you for your kindness to him. It finds me in the midst of hard work. I have got to finish February & work these Eastern cities, & it is not easy, besides, I am about arranging a 4 weeks Southern tour of Mr. Beecher, which will pay me something. He is to start the middle of February. If I have to go with you & Mark, it leaves me at the end of Feb. with nothing. I have never done so much work in my life since I was 21 years of age that paid me so little considering the amount of business done. I have had to watch every move & get all that possibly could be got out of the tour. I have had a good deal of pride in it, & have worked to make it what it has proven, a grand success.

Now can't you & Mark get on with a perfectly honest, industrious man, who would be your slave, who only has to take care of you & to settle the houses. Ed. traveled two weeks with Mr. Beecher. He was careful and took good care—"good care!!!" of Mr. & Mrs. Beecher & he can of you & Mark, & I can finish up the work East. If I go away during Feb. I can do nothing but take care of you and Mark & the other business has to be neglected. It is all one night business & speculative. No sales. I want to fill your time for March if I can, & I want to see if some-

52

thing cannot be planned for next season. I have so much to make me blue that I was taken sick this morning & had to go to bed. Well, what's the use! I had a note from Mrs. Cable yesterday, & I am looking for a servant for her. I also sent her $25. yesterday, as she wrote me she would like it. I will send her $25. more to-day. Oh, how I wish I could leave my business to fly to Ozias. Love to dear Mark.[79]

This letter seems to have provoked a scorching telegram from Twain, but so desperately did Pond cling to his perch in New York that he tried one more plaintive letter to Cable, written on February 2:

I have been so upset by Ozias illness that I am absolutely sick. Mark's telegram is very severe & takes the pluck out of me. I dont ask him to take on inexperienced men. He can have as good a man as there is in the country. My records show how I have worked. This has been my favorite schem [sic]. I have worked seven months on this business & I have received $2100, & Mark $1200 [$12,000?]. & you $4,000 a [illegible], & I have got to make arrangements for something beyond. Mr. Beecher would have gone South in Feb. but I could not possibly book the time. He has set March 1st to start & if Mark insists that no one but myself will do then I lose the only chance I have to make my summer expenses. I have never done so much for so little money when there has been such a fine business, as I have the past Seven months. I just wish you could see the amount of work it has required. I dont complain, but I do feel that Mark ought not to ask me to sacrifice my whole prospect, especially when I can be more value where I am, & any good honest man can settle when contracts are already made & all business done before you arrive in a town. I enclose a letter which I wish you would read & if you *think* best give to Mark, & if *not* best dont—I love him & dont want to do wrong, but I must live for the sake of those depending on me.[80]

In Milwaukee, where he stayed quietly until February 18, when he departed for New York, Ozias had no doubt that his brother would rejoin the tour in Chicago as requested, and that is what Major Pond seems to have done.

There was also no doubt in Ozias' mind that he had been touring with great men. He recorded in his diary his gratitude to Twain and Cable for their care of him during his illness. Cable, he wrote in Milwaukee on January 29,

53

is the most perfect man that it has ever been my good fortune to meet. He has the courage of his convictions and will make his influence felt in this land if his health is spared, which, Heaven grant. It would be but a poor return for me to enter in this humble journal, my thanks and heartfelt gratitude to Messrs. Clemens and Cable for their thoughtful care and kindness to me on the latter part of this trip, when my health is so rapidly declining. . . . For Mr. Cable, let me say, that I have never known a kinder, nobler, manlier man, and for the beautiful words he has written in memory of my sainted mother, may Heaven bless him throughout his noble, useful life.

Mr. Clemens has a heart as tender as a child's; as loving as a woman. He dreads to look upon suffering, but cannot hide the sympathy he feels for those who are affected, and although one unacquainted with him might think him almost totally indifferent to such matters, the close observer can always see the sadness in his eyes and the aching heart, when human suffering is brought within his sight. I shall never forget his quaint, kind ways, and shall always love him as one most desiring *the love of his friends.*

Mr. Cable sat in my room, read and talked to me in the most gentle and kindly way. He would not allow people to see me. He has been so good.

For some weeks Clemens, Cable, and Ozias had been using the "quaint" language of Malory "in the cars and hotels."[81] (After immersing himself in the copy of the *Morte d'Arthur* that he bought in Rochester on December 6, Twain wrote from Grand Rapids, Michigan, on December 14 to order Charley Webster to get a copy for Ozias, then in New York.)[82] Now he and Cable, having moved on from Milwaukee, signed themselves to a telegram sent to cheer Ozias as Sir Mark Twain and Sir George W. Cable:

Now wit you well, Sir Sagramore, thou Knight and gentle; that there be two that right wonderly do love thee, grieving passing sore at thy heavy travail. And we will meet [*sic*] that thou prosper at the hand of the leech and come lightly forth of thy hurts and be as thou were tofore.

Ozias explained in his diary that he had been dubbed "Sir Sagramore, Knight of the Lake," but Mark informed Livy—risking a shocked rejoinder—that Ozias was called "Sir Sagramore le Desirous."[83]

54

On January 31 Clemens and Cable read in Davenport, Iowa, to an audience of about one thousand. Clemens gave one of his stock interviews to the reporter from the *Democrat*.[84] That night, after the reading, Twain took a train for Chicago, apparently headquarters for the troupe until February 4. Before leaving Davenport he had a disagreement with Cable, who was unwilling to start for Chicago until Monday morning, as otherwise he would have been compelled to travel on the Sabbath. Twain boiled over and continued to boil for most of the rest of the tour. He complained to J. B. Pond and, possibly at this time, wrote him a note in which he damned Cable as "a Christ-besprinkled psalm-singing Presbyterian."[85] On February 5 he blew off steam to Livy in a letter from South Bend:

I do not believe that any vileness, any shame, any dishonor is too base for Cable to do, provided by doing it he can save his despicable Sabbath from abrasion. In him this superstition is lunacy—no idiocy—pure & unadulterated. Apart from this & his colossal self-conceit & avarice, he is all great & fine: but *with* them as ballast, he averages as other men & floats upon an even keel with the rest.[86]

He complained of his companion again on the sixth in a letter dated from Lafayette, Indiana. In another long, violent letter written on February 9, after a Sunday layover in Indianapolis, he took the same tone but added another item to the charges against Cable. Here Twain said that he had been able to modify somewhat Cable's insulting and insolent ways with servants but had not managed to cure him. Pond, he added, observed that the servants at Everett House, in New York, all hated Cable and that Cable starved himself when he was paying his own expenses and was insatiable when someone else paid.[87]

On February 3 they read in Detroit, Major Pond being back with the show to handle business arrangements. On Wednesday, the fourth, they read in South Bend. The way was paved by the usual advertisement in the *Daily Times* from January 30 through February 3 and by advertisements accompanied by a photograph in the *Evening Register* for

February 2 through 4. A special announcement in the *Times* for February 1 prophesied that South Bend had never before had so fine a feast of reason or humor or so splendid an elocutionary treat. The *Evening Register* for the second carried a facetious story about its photograph of the performers:

The handsome portraits of Mr. Samuel L. Clemens (Mark Twain), and Mr. George W. Cable, produced in this issue of The Register should have appeared in the Sunday edition. Our engraver gives his excuse for not having the plates ready that in putting on the finishing touches his engraving tool slipped and cut off one of Mr. Clemens' ears. The engraver had on hand a cut of two prize-fighters that were splendid portraits of the two lecturers, but owing to the fact that they were presented in fighting postures and stripped to the waist, the engraving was not used in the place of the spoiled one, lest it might attract a crowd to the opera-house to see a prize fight instead of a select audience to listen to a literary entertainment as is desired. It was too late Saturday night to arrange for a railroad accident whereby Mark Twain might lose an ear to correspond with the cut, so there was no other way than to postpone presenting the pleasing faces until the current edition of The Register.

The editor then heightened his jest by introducing his own version of a story about a map of Paris which Twain engraved during the Franco-Prussian War. Twain's tool slipped, and the only way to use the plate was to change the course of the river Seine. This Twain did "as a dernier resort, and it came dernier resulting in his being discharged."

The third South Bend newspaper, the *Daily Tribune,* quoted in its issue for February 2 the review from the Boston *Globe* of November 14 which Pond seems to have sent out regularly with his advance publicity.

All three newspapers presented pedestrian reviews of the performance in their issues for February 5. The critic for the *Times* considered "Mary's Night Ride" far the best of Cable's numbers but found himself unable to discriminate among Twain's; the critic for the *Register* contrasted the broad humor of Twain and the refined wit and tender pathos of Cable; and the critic for the *Tribune* was impressed by the pleasing incongruity between the two speakers.

56

Making their second stand in Indianapolis, the entertainers performed three times on February 6 and 7 and remained through Sunday, the eighth. On the ninth, Twain blasted Cable in a scorching letter to Livy.[88] The next day he poured out more wrath in another letter home,[89] expostulating because Cable blandly read the same old selections after announcing to newspapers that he would read new ones. Worse still, Cable read the same selections repeatedly in the same places — five times in Chicago and three times in Indianapolis. Worst of all, the selection called "Mary's Night Ride" had crept up from six minutes in New Haven to fifteen minutes and now appeared in *every* program. "Cover the child"— one of Cable's climactic lines—was increasingly hard for Twain to stomach, and years later it stood in the minds of Clemens and his wife for the bathetic or melodramatic.[90] Clemens asserted broodingly that he contemplated dropping another of Cable's pieces from the program. A saving circumstance was that Clemens felt that he, himself, had at last learned his trade: he made the people in Columbus shout and "tore them all to pieces."

The newspaper record of the reading in Columbus suggests that Twain was correct in thinking that he was enthusiastically received but wrong in feeling that Cable was not liked. The reading was well advertised in the Columbus *Evening Dispatch*. Pond placed an announcement and a photograph of the two readers in the paper for February 9. The management of Comstock's Opera House listed the reading in several issues, along with other coming attractions. The proposed program was printed on February 6, and on February 9 a squib appeared under "Amusements" to the effect that a crowded house would be well entertained that night.

Writing on Tuesday, February 10, the critic was as delighted with the performance as was Twain himself. The audience was "magnificent in size and character." The most ardent anticipations were realized, and the severest critics satisfied. Twain's presence, voice, looks, and manner gave expression and added force to his humor, which was, in fact, transformed into reality and life by the magic of voice and countenance.

57

Cable was said to be equally original and pleasing in his part of the program. The contrast between the two readers was "a most agreeable feature of the dual performance." Furthermore, "Mary's Night Ride" was "extremely good." All told, the readings formed an epoch in the history of amusements in the city.

In Oberlin, Ohio, the Union Library Association sponsored readings given in the First Congregational Church on February 11. Cable read from *Dr. Sevier,* and Twain gave the crowd his "King Sollermun," "The Tragic Tale of a Fishwife," "A Trying Situation," and a few shorter selections. The audience was cool, and the *Weekly News* charged that Twain had humbugged and swindled the people of Oberlin, who, it seems, expected readings to combine the improving with the pleasing. The program director for the Union Library Association replied apologetically that although Twain's reading was not exactly what was expected, it was satisfactory "as entertainment." Fourteen years later, when Twain published "The Man That Corrupted Hadleyburg," citizens of Oberlin thought that their town was the prototype for Hadleyburg and that the writer was taking belated revenge for a bad press.[91]

Twain had a number of failures as lecturer and reader during his long career, but reviews indicate that audiences during this tour were, for the most part, enthusiastic. Mark always took his lecturing and reading seriously. He exulted over a good performance and fretted after a bad one. Preparation for the readings took precedence over social engagements. After a reading on the night of February 12 in Detroit, he wrote to George Iles, a friend in Montreal, refusing for Cable and himself an invitation from the Tuque Bleue Snowshoe Club[92] to join in an excursion across Mount Royal. Both readers needed to be abed, he explained, in order to be prepared for talking. A ghastly dullness settled down upon him on the platform if he lacked rest, and his cast-iron duty was to his audience.[93]

The Detroit performance was given a blunt, apt review in the *Post* for February 13:

The "Mark Twain"-Cable readings drew a large audience to Whitney's last night, a good proportion being composed of those who enjoyed the readings of the two authors here in December last. Of the two Mr. Cable is not near as good a raconteur as Mr. Clemens, although he assumes much more of the manner of the professional elocutionist. Mr. Cable's selection most pleasing and most applauded was "Mary's Night Ride," which was narrated in a graphic manner. He sang, too, the negro boat and love songs admirably. "Mark Twain"—he should petition the legislature to legally entitle him to wear his nom de plume for every day use—has that peculiar sense of humor so dear to the American heart, which finds expression in the wildest flights of mendacity, or in a gentle burlesquing of the truth. His manner heightens the effect of everything he says, because it seems to be utterly unfitted for public readings, and yet it is thoroughly artistic, and entirely appropriate to whatever character he represents as speaking. . .

Only second-flight society could have attended this reading, for February 12 was the night of the grand levee given for Governor Alger by the Detroit Light Guard. The occasion was described as brilliant, with Michigan's elite mingling in a scene of gaiety.

Possibly the real feature of the reading at Whitney's was Cable's departure from routine to offer selections from *The Grandissimes* ("Raoul Innerarity Exhibits His Paintings"; "Raoul Innerarity Announces His Marriage"; and "Amore and Honore—Courtship Scene").

Unlike the *Post,* the *Free Press* for February 14 gave the performance a most perfunctory notice but made up for its apparent inattention by printing on Sunday, February 15, a long, heavily comic interview by "Luke Sharp" under the heading "The Re-Mark-Able Twain":

The city editor said to me Thursday, as he handed me his theater pass:
"Most of the boys have to be at the Governor's ball to-night and I wish you would take in the Twain-Cable entertainment."
"I thought the Russell House had taken them in and entertained them. At least they'll think they were taken in when they see the bill."
"If you see Maj. Pond," continued the city editor, "just apologize to him and say that I'd have sent up somebody that knew

59

something if it were not for the Governor's snap. Tell him everybody that amounts to anything is on duty there. Try and get it into some sort of shape now. Begin it 'Whitney's.' If there is a good crowd, it's a 'large and enthusiastic audience.' If there's only a few, it's a 'small but appreciative audience.' "

The reporter found Major Pond, entered into a humorously confusing conversation with him, evaded the guard set to keep him from the theater, and engaged in conversation with Twain and Cable when they came in:

Twain took off a fur muffler that was round his neck and stamped up and down the room a bit to see if he still had the use of himself after the cold walk. Cable also shed his wraps and adjusted his white necktie before the glass. Southerner as he was, he didn't seem to feel the cold as much as the Northern author.

Then Mark took a look at the audience. Coming back he said:
"The Governor's got 'em, Cable."
"Again!"
"He's got the audience, I mean. We'll have to talk to empty benches, I'm afraid."
"It's not 8 o'clock yet," said Cable. And it wasn't. Before the hour struck the house was well filled.

The reporter announced to Twain that he was there for an interview, and Twain pointed out that he would be available only in sections. The interview continued, then, in sections, first with Twain, next with Cable, as the performers alternated on the platform. Cable is described as having a silky black beard and a long, twisted moustache with ends hanging down below his chin, making a bow over his mouth. "His nose is straight and small, his eyes bright, black and piercing, and his forehead high. His hair is the color of jet, and as glossy as oiled ebony."

The story ends with a return to the stereotyped comedy of its beginning as the reporter hands his article to the city editor:

"What's all this?" said the city editor when I handed it to him.
"The Twain-Cable critique."
"Critique! What did they do?"
"Do? Why, they gave selections from—"
"What selections?"

60

"Those down on the programme, of course."

"Where's the programme?"

"Here in my pocket."

"Well, why in thunder don't you give it. This is as bad as a fire without the insurance."

"Now, look here. Every one there had a programme. They were free. Those people don't want to know. Those who were not there are not interested or they would have been there."

"Yes, but hang it—"

"If *you* want to know, Cable gave two selections about Raoul Innerarity, sang some Creole songs—greatly applauded—and recited most graphically 'Mary's Night Ride Through the Southern Lines.'

"Twain gave his desperate encounter with an interviewer, Tom Sawyer, the prejudiced cat, Huck. Finn, made a speech—"

"Made a speech!! And, great Caesar, you haven't a word of it? Don't you know—was there no child there that could tell you?— that anything a man like Twain says is of the utmost importance."

"If you heard him talk as much as I did you wouldn't say that. He said that he supposed they were all anxious to get to the Governor's levee, and they laughed. He said he hated to keep them, but if they liked he would tell them a short story and then they might escape. He told the story—about the incorporated Company of Mean Men, who docked the man who was blown up because he lost time. Then he—Mark Twain—came back, and as the audience insisted on it gave them 'The Jumping Frog.' That was all. There was a large audience, and they were awfully well pleased."

The city man wearily handed back the copy, and said:

"You may want to keep this as a memento of the reading. I should have sent the elevator boy."

Their excursion into Canada assumed glorious festival aspects. On Friday, February 13, the men read in London, Ontario, and the next day visited Helmuth Female College. Tobogganing with the girls proved a thrilling sport. That night they arrived in Toronto after dark, a change in schedule having made them fail in an exciting dash for the train they had intended to take. On Sunday both men wrote enthusiastic letters home about their experiences with the girls on Saturday.[94] From Toronto their itinerary took them eastward across Canada to Brockville,[95] to Ottawa, where they read on February 17, and to Montreal. Despite the beauty of winter in Canada Twain continued to nurse his irritation

61

at Cable. He informed Livy on the seventeenth that his companion was the "pitifulest human louse" he had ever known.[96]

Mark's feelings were probably not improved by the critique in the London *Advertizer* for February 14. The reporter called Cable the "most artistic" of the two and thought Twain a man capable of playing high comedy but aware that there is more money in doing a song and dance.

At Ottawa the readers were the cause of dissension in the Commons, then in session. Mr. Charlton, "a prominent member of the opposition," intimated to the Premier that an adjournment to permit members to attend the readings would be acceptable. When the house objected to the adjournment, "Sir John called across the floor to Mr. Charlton, 'You'll not be an "Innocent Abroad" tonight.' "[97]

Twain's festering canker apparently remained unknown to Cable, and for him Canada continued to have a holiday air only. He was charmed with Montreal, their headquarters for February 18, 19, and 20. He enjoyed snow, ice statuary, winter costumes, furs, sleighs, and healthy young people turning winter into a game.

Montreal knew Twain for a genuine lion. The newspapers quoted from his new book *(The Adventures of Huckleberry Finn)*, published his photograph and a letter, and noticed his performances in detail. The Athenæum Club, a fashionable literary society, gave the men a brilliant reception at the Windsor hotel from 4:30 until after 6:00 on the afternoon of Wednesday, February 18. About five hundred "leading citizens" were invited and some two hundred, most of them women, were "presented" to the novelists. A discreet orchestra played softly, while club members and their guests chatted with the voluble Mr. Clemens and the polite Mr. Cable. The *Gazette,* the *Daily Star,* and the *Herald and Daily Commercial Gazette* added long lists of those who attended to their notices published on February 19.

The *Gazette* and the *Star* reviewed at length the reading at the Queen's Hall on the night of February 18 in their issues for the following day. The *Gazette* thought that there had been no event in which the public had taken such interest as in the tour of Clemens and Cable since "the immortal Charles Dickens delighted the English speaking people of the old and new world":

There is only one Mark Twain in the world who can write such genuine fun. Those who saw the performance last evening may come to the conclusion there is only one who can really be a true exponent of that fun, and that man is Mark Twain himself. Nearly as much can be said for the distinguished novelist, Mr. Cable. . . . few writers can appear before an audience and electrify and delight it by readings from the works of their own pen. Mr. Cable can do this, and in a manner which cannot be rivaled.

The *Star* was similarly approving. It held Twain's fun to be inimitable, the pleasure derived from reading his work being nothing when compared to that of hearing the great author himself; and Cable presented his humor and pathos perfectly.

After the performance on the eighteenth, the troupe drove at headlong speed out of the snow-covered city to the home of the Tuque Bleue Snowshoe Club. Husky young club members seized Clemens, Cable and the huge major and tossed them repeatedly to the ceiling. Each of the visitors made speeches, Cable sang "Pov' Piti Momzel Zizi,"[98] club members sang a snowshoe song, and, finally, all joined in "God Save the Queen."[99]

To review a second performance was not standard practice, but the *Gazette*, the *Star*, and the *Herald* all published full critiques on February 20. The hall, they agreed, was, if anything, more crowded than it had been for the first performance. Both men were again excellent. Cable's voice was clear, sweet, and well-modulated, whether reading or singing. His vivid description of Congo Plains, later Congo Square, and his singing of the invitation to the Kun-ye dance, of "Susette, You Don't Love Me," and of "Zizi" were all much applauded. Twain held his readers under a species of fascination from the moment when he stumbled on the stage, passed his hand through his frizzled hair, and drawled: "Ladies and gentlemen, a great many of you here present have had a good deal to do with boys, and the rest of you have been boys."

63

The party left Canada on the twentieth and read that night in Saratoga. On Saturday, the twenty-first, in New York, the returned travelers held something like a family reunion at breakfast with Ozias and Ozias' wife, Nella. Cable showed proper interest in Ozias' improvement, and Twain presented him with a copy of the newly published *Huck Finn*. In New York the lecturers girded themselves for the last few days of their tour. They appeared in Philadelphia on the twenty-sixth, in Baltimore on the twenty-seventh, and in Washington — their last stop — on Saturday, the twenty-eighth.

V. Personalities

ALTHOUGH the bitter epithets that Clemens applied to Cable are not to be dismissed as the result of a temporary dyspepsia, their importance may easily be exaggerated. Writing in Baltimore, Twain attempted a judicial estimate of Cable. He addressed to Howells what was, for him, a rational, objective report:

To-night in Baltimore, to-morrow afternoon and night in Washington, and my four-months platform campaign is ended at last. It has been a curious experience. It has taught me that Cable's gifts of mind are greater and higher than I had suspected. But—

That "But" is pointing toward his religion. You will never, never know, never divine, guess, imagine, how loathsome a thing the Christian religion can be made until you come to know and study Cable daily and hourly. Mind you, I like him; he is pleasant company; I rage and swear at him sometimes, but we do not quarrel; we get along mighty happily together; but in him and his person I have learned to hate all religions. He has taught me to abhor and detest the Sabbath-day and hunt up new and troublesome ways to dishonor it.[100]

Twain's opinion of Cable was both complex and shifting. Twain was an emotional whirligig who could, nevertheless, retain a grudge or an ill opinion. In addition to detesting Cable's annoying, ritualistic pieties, he complained of two other major vices: Cable was a miser; and Cable read too long and with too theatrical a manner.

64

Twain habitually felt that his business associates robbed him. Perhaps Cable's holding out for $450.00 a week instead of the first proffered $350.00 soured the trip for Twain before it began. Certainly Cable's small economies and habit of charging to general expenses what Twain considered personal items came close to setting off an explosion.

What truth there was in Twain's adverse reflections on Cable as a reader may not be clearly established from other available evidence;[101] yet it must be acknowledged that Twain was a discriminating judge of speakers and readers. He demanded something approaching perfection both of himself and of others; and he approved a carefully rehearsed but "natural" presentation. He liked Cable's early, easy, drawing-room performances; but he thought that under the tutelage of elocutionists Cable acquired a distressingly artificial delivery. This was not his initial reaction, however; a year before they toured together he wrote that Cable, who had been "training under an expert," was "just a rattling reader—the best amateur I ever heard; & with 2 seasons of *public* practice I guess he'll be the best professional reader alive."[102] Thirty years later Howells, to whom Clemens thus praised Cable, said that the little novelist was, in his own way, "as fine a performer as Clemens."[103] On December 9 [?], 1884, Twain, in one of his happier moods, wrote to Livy from Toronto in praise of Cable:

Tonight we had a noble hall to talk in, and an audience befitting it. Both of us had a gorgeously good time. I saw ladies swabbing their eyes freely and undisguisedly after Cable's "Night Ride." He did it well.[104]

But throughout much of the tour Mark expressed a strong distaste for Cable's affected voice, lingering pathos, and drawn-out selections. Shortly after the end of the tour he complimented Howells on his success as a reader and seized the opportunity to contrast it with Cable's artificiality:

Heiliger Gott! but it was good reading. Far better than Cable could have done it—which is not much of a compliment, but it started honestly *out* to be a compliment. It had simplicity, sincerity, & absence of artificiality, in place of Cable's self-compla-

cency, sham feeling & labored artificiality. Sincerity *is* a great & valuable thing in front of an audience. . . . But you couldn't read worth a damn a few years ago. . . .
P. S. Cable's response to Pond, on the International Copyright invitation was eminently characteristic—to this effect: If they want me to read, let them pay my price.

He is intellectually great—very great, I think—but in order to find room for this greatness in his pygmy carcase, God had to cramp his other qualities more than was judicious, it seems to me.[105]

A little later he wrote to Howells again:

I have been giving myself a 24-hours' cursing for never thinking until yesterday of trying to bribe you to take Cable's empty place & help me read here to-night. We could have had such a good time! & I could retire to the ante-room with such tranquil confidence that you would charm & delight the house instead of extorting from them their damnable compassion.[106]

In 1907, looking back across the years, he dictated a milder indictment of his partner's ability:

Cable had been scouting the country alone for three years with readings from his novels, and he had been a good reader in the beginning for he had been born with a natural talent for it, but unhappily he prepared himself for his public work by taking lessons from a teacher of elocution, and so by the time he was ready to begin his platform work he was so well and thoroughly educated that he was merely theatrical and artificial and not half as pleasing and entertaining to a house as he had been in the splendid days of his ignorance.[107]

Ten years after the tour, in a benevolent mood, Mark wrote in genial phrases that serve as a legitimate counterweight to the overwrought epithets provoked during the tour:

. . . Yes sir! I liked you in spite of your religion; & I always said to myself that a man that could be good & kindly with that kind of a load on him was entitled to homage—& I *paid* it. And I have always said, & still maintain, that as a railroad-comrade you were perfect—the only railroad-comrade in the world that a man of moods & frets & uncertainties of disposition could travel with, a third of a year, and never weary of his company. We *always* had good times in the cars, & never minded the length of the trips—& my, but they *were* sockdolagers for length![108]

66

Although Twain and Pond incautiously aired their griev-
ances at the end of the tour,[109] Cable — Twain's miserly little
human louse — seems to have continued always in the supposition that he and Clemens were very nearly kindred souls,
barring trivial disagreements about religion and profanity.
During the tour he enjoyed Mark's company enough to pur-
sue him into the smoking compartments on the train. Knowing Cable's prejudices, Twain once asked why he chose to sit
where smoking and profanity were customary, and Cable
answered, "I know Mark, I don't do these things, but I can't
help admiring the way you do them."[110] When he went on
solitary engagements a few weeks after separating from
Clemens, the little novelist wrote almost pathetically to his
wife, "It comes hard reading alone — without Mark, I
mean."[111]

Upon reflection, one sees some justification for Cable's
feeling of intellectual kinship. Both Twain and Cable had
broken with a culture and had the hard problem of discover-
ing or creating a new culture for themselves. They were close
together on many important points of social doctrine. Both
hated social injustice with the ardor of crusaders. And although Twain may never have known it, Cable was not im-
mutably fixed in the annoying evangelical conventions and
ritual that he had been trained in. During these first years in
the East Cable was, in fact, rapidly recovering from his
provincial puritanism. Before he died he went to plays freely,
conceded that cards were not hell-inspired, took a drink of
whisky when in the bosom of his family, and traveled on
Sunday. As he became more economically secure, he may have
loosened his grip on money. But even in these later years
Twain would not have been completely satisfied with him,
for he never learned to use profanity or to play billiards.

VI. The Adventures of Huckleberry Finn

THE RESULTS of the tour were varied and important, though somewhat difficult to list and assess. Cable gained money and experience; Twain earned money that streamed through his fingers. Both men wanted advertising for their books, and they did obtain excellent publicity. Reporters dogged their steps and hung on Twain's words, on and off the platform: a fabulously vital, dynamic quality in the man made news of everything he did or said at this stage in his career.[112] Association with him brought Cable into prominence and improved his status as speaker and writer if not as a social thinker. Practice in reading was highly beneficial to Cable, but it was also useful to Twain, who had often lectured but who had done little public reading from his works.

The tour and associations before the tour began had other consequences. These may well have been the most exciting months of Cable's life. During them he reached the peak of his fame as an artist and published his most significant work on civil rights. His intellectual and social horizons were enlarging rapidly during his early months in the North and East, and he undoubtedly learned a lot from Twain, who was possessed of a disorderly but fascinating mind, a persuasive tongue, and a wealth of strong opinions and dubious information. But unfortunately, by May, 1881, Cable's best fiction was behind him; he never managed to exploit a new vein or to rework the old successfully, and whatever influence Twain may have had on him is more interesting to the biographer than to the critic. On the other hand, the problem of Cable's influence on Twain becomes an important though elusive one for the critic, for Twain had some of his best work before him.

During the tour there occurred one widely reported incident that has obvious, if superficial, bearing on Twain's work. When Twain fingered Malory's *Morte d'Arthur* in a second-hand book store, Cable praised the work and interested

68

Twain in it.[113] That Cable may, on this account, be thought of as providing the initial cause for *The Connecticut Yankee* fixes on him a responsibility which does not seem as important now, except perhaps for Hollywood, as it once did. More important and more interesting is the possibility that Cable's frank recognition of sex as a human and literary motive and of miscegenation as a tragic theme may have emboldened Clemens to make what is, among his writings, a conspicuously serious approach to sex problems in *Pudd'nhead Wilson*. Most important is the possibility that Cable may have exerted a fundamental influence on the view of society that permeates *The Adventures of Huckleberry Finn*.

Here is a fascinating but, for lack of definite information, highly speculative topic. One kind of influence that has been suggested previously may be dismissed as unimportant and almost positively mistaken. This is the supposition that Twain may have made detailed, verbal revisions of his manuscript to accord with suggestions from Cable, who is said to have been his guest at Hartford while the book "was being prepared for the press."[114] Bernard DeVoto, who observes that Cable had "an infinitely timorous mind," is here thinking of the kind of bowdlerizing that is attributed to such genteel critics as Olivia Clemens and Richard Watson Gilder.[115]

Available evidence does not support the conjecture that Cable, or, indeed, anyone else, induced Twain to expurgate drastically the text of *Huck Finn*. Studies of the extant manuscript pages indicate that the many changes made were for the most part the revisions of a craftsman rather than the censorious changes of a timid editor.[116] Howells, Olivia Clemens, and Clemens himself are usually supposed to have been responsible for the revisions, except for modifications made by Gilder in chapters published in the *Century*.

That Olivia Clemens was responsible for a good many of the changes made is very likely. The summer of 1883, when Twain composed the greater part of *Huck Finn*, was one of those periods during which Livy and the two older girls, Susy and Clara, edited Twain's manuscript each day as he wrote it. To supply amusement for himself and the girls, Twain says that often, when he was writing, he "interlarded remarks of a studied and felicitously atrocious character" and pretended to object to having them deleted, only to strike them out privately if Olivia weakened in her editorial purpose.[117] It is also clear that Howells recommended some verbal changes when he read proof on part of the book in August, 1884.[118]

Our knowledge of the times when Cable visited the Clemenses or read the proof sheets of *Huck Finn* does not support the assumption that he, too, was responsible for detailed changes. Cable paid brief visits to Clemens in Hartford in October and November, 1882, lectured and read in Hartford in 1883 (but did not stay with the Clemenses), and remained, because of illness, in Clemens' house from about January 26 to February 15, 1884.[119] He did not read proof sheets on *Huck Finn* until October, 1884.

Now, in October and November, 1882, and in April, 1883, the story of Huck Finn seems to have been completely in suspense; in January and February, 1884, the book was finished, arrangements for its publication were in progress, and Clemens was occupied with plays that he was writing or had just written. Proof sheets were not ready, it seems, until sometime in July, 1884. Up until October, 1884, after *Huck Finn* had passed through a variety of editorial hands, Cable does not seem to have had any convenient opportunity for recommending changes of any kind. Furthermore, neither he nor Clemens mentions anywhere that he had any part in revising either manuscript or proofs. What Cable does write confirms that when he read the proofs he simply was looking for passages suitable for use on the platform.

Cable's influence on *Huck Finn* must have been general and pervasive rather than specific, indirect rather than direct, and early rather than late. This does not mean that, if given an opportunity, Cable would not have supported Livy in her softenings of Mark's language. But he would not have supported her or her husband in their inclination to shy away from some of the subjects that frightened them. Cable adhered to many fundamentalist notions and practices approved by southern Presbyterians of his day, but on large social questions—even on miscegenation—his ideas were logical, firm, and astoundingly bold.

It is my opinion that Twain was strongly influenced by Cable, much more in 1881-83 than in 1884-85 (when Mark had taken a dislike to certain of Cable's habits and biases), and that Cable's influence had to do with ideas, not choice of language.

Cable may have influenced *Huck Finn* significantly with respect to its social and poetic attitudes at points where Twain explores the nature of culture and the nature of men's relationships within a culture. With exceptional imaginative intensity, Twain presents in *Huck Finn* simple but fundamental symbols — like the great, flowing river — and complex, symbolic situations in which the life of the slave seems idyllic, noble, and free and the life of the owner insecure and fettered, in which a white boy enjoys sexless love poured forth by a black slave with the uncomplicated bounteousness that a romantic mind might attribute to benign Nature. Such deep-lying symbols and vividly imagined relationships have peculiar value and power because, in this one book, Twain frames them concretely in a civilization both warmly felt and adequately analyzed.

Twain's perceptive nerve endings were delicately aquiver at nearly all times; he did not need to be sensitized. But thought gives direction to feeling, and Twain did need help in grasping intellectually through an analysis of the morphology of Southern society what he felt to be its unhealthy moral state. He had to have an orientation quite different from that of his youth before he could arrive at penetrating insights and form ripe judgments.[120] His adult, discriminating attitude, gained no matter how, gives extraordinary affective power to his social insights in *The Adventures of Huckleberry Finn*. Bernard DeVoto observes that the prime difference between *Tom Sawyer* and *Huck Finn* is that in the later book Twain brings mature judgment to bear on prewar Mississippi Valley society. "Society is passed through the mind of a boy, as be-

71

fore, but this time there is a man of fifty speaking."[121]

Twain was not a boy, however, when he finished *Tom Sawyer;* he was forty years old. Yet the difference between the two books is clear. *Tom Sawyer* is idyllic and nostalgic; the four hundred motiveless pages of *Huck Finn* that Twain wrote in the summer of 1876 likewise exploit the themes of pastoralism, nostalgia, superstition, and terror.[122] But *Huck Finn* as completed, with much of the earlier work eliminated, is not merely a continuation of *Tom Sawyer*. Twain supplies a narrative purpose and an ethical theme that make the parts of the book cohere, and he is brilliantly analytic and judicial in the view of society implicit in language and action.

We must not permit Mr. DeVoto to cancel one shrewd observation with a second, the partly unfortunate suggestion that Twain was "imprisoned in his boyhood."[123] The two observations must be synthesized: Twain's selective memory of his boyhood gave him a simplified, poetic world where, in writing *Huck Finn*, withdrawn from but still cognizant of the ugly confusions of society, he could puzzle critically over questions of freedom and responsibility, of codified ethics and natural ethics, of psychic fear, courage, hypocrisy, and love. The unanswered question is, how did Twain happen to combine in *Huck Finn* a mature social view and an aesthetic balance that he failed to achieve before or afterwards? The answer may not be patly given, if at all, but it has to do, in part at least, with unusual immediate circumstances. His trip on the Mississippi during the spring of 1882 served to freshen and make vivid his memories of the river and of the river country — not that his images of his boyhood and of his favorite objects of imitation were ever much less than eidetic. But that the full vigor of his mature intelligence should be brought to bear during a literary re-exploration of the society of the Mississippi Valley requires explanation. The total influence of William Dean Howells as a critic of society should not be overlooked, but Howells did not know the South. Cable did know the South, and his opinions were of just the proper kind to whet Twain's critical faculties.

Although Cable could hardly have been active in censor-

72

ing *Huck Finn,* he was in a strategic position to exercise a broad influence on Mark's ideas during a period of two years immediately preceding the summer when Twain composed the major part of the book.[124] Twain had read some of Cable's work before early summer of 1881 and thought so highly of what he had read that when Cable visited Hartford on June 13, Mark and Mrs. Clemens took the train "from somewhere beyond New Haven" in order to meet the Louisiana writer and to have lunch with him.[125] Correspondence followed.

Twain's revisiting the Mississippi in the spring of 1882 has been identified repeatedly as an emotionally stimulating, fecundating experience; that the fertilizing effect was intellectual as well as emotional needs to be stressed. When Clemens and Osgood, after a wonderful trip down the river, arrived in New Orleans in April, 1882, they visited Cable's home as his established friends and out of their carefully husbanded time spent one afternoon and two stimulating evenings there. Twain, who had the habits of a reporter, was absorbing as much as he could of what southern writers were saying about the South. Joel Chandler Harris was one of the writers who interested him; so he persuaded Harris to take the train from Atlanta to New Orleans to meet him for a visit. Like Cable, Harris was a southerner with ideas on proper relationships between literature and society. Something of the bent of his thoughts is indicated by his editorials on southern literature. The demand for fiction in defense of the South — which accompanied a call for southern literature — caught his attention:

. . . Whether this is owing to the lack of healthy criticism or to the fact that we have been put upon the defensive so long that anything in relation to the South, its conditions or its institutions, past or present, which is suspiciously critical or even severely impartial, is construed into an attack, we have not time here to consider. We suspect, however, that it is due, rather, to the social and political isolation in which the South sought to preserve its peculiar property investment. It is natural that such isolation should produce remarkable pride of opinion and a belief that our civilization was perfect.[126]

Genuine artists, he felt, will be too impartial to suit those who have grown fat through feeding upon the romantic idea that no additional polish could be put upon southern perfection. In another editorial Harris distinguished between local and sectional literature. "The very spice and essence of all literature, the very marrow and essence of all literary art is its localism." But the man to make proper use of local materials will feel that his work is belittled if it is claimed on the score of sectionalism. "We have no Southern literature worthy of the name, because an attempt has been made to give it the peculiarities of sectionalism rather than to impart to it the flavor of localism." It was along such lines that Cable was arguing in 1881-83.

When Harris and Twain came together at Cable's home, Twain took delight in reading aloud from *Uncle Remus* and from his own works.[127] Cable read aloud, also, and the three men must have enjoyed a feeling of close, provincial comradeship in the world of creative enterprise. They were all gifted southerners expressing the South as they saw it: beautiful, delicate, brave; slovenly, coarse, and barbarous.

There is no question about the immediate attraction that Cable had for Twain. When Cable visited the Clemenses in Hartford in October and November, 1882, Twain was again fascinated by him. After the latter visit he wrote to Howells that Cable created worshippers on all hands and was a marvelous talker on a deep subject. He did not see how even Herbert Spencer could "unwind a thought more smoothly or orderly," and do it in cleaner, crisper English. As for moral honesty, limpid innocence, and blemishless piety, the Apostles were mere policemen to him.[128]

It was not until Cable fell ill in the Clemens home in January, 1884, that Twain's admiration was clouded over. Meanwhile, during the summer of 1883, Mark had completed *Huckleberry Finn*.

Late in June, 1883, the Clemens family retired to Quarry Farm, the country home near Elmira, New York, of Olivia Clemens' adopted sister, Mrs. Theodore Crane. Here Twain's fertile, freakish fancy devised plots and motifs for stories, most of them extravagant and worthless. He worked enthusiastically (even while writing *Huckleberry Finn*) on "1002," a long, dull burlesque of the *Arabian Nights*. Sometime in July, it seems, after an intermission of seven years, he fell upon his old Huck Finn manuscript.[129] His "tank," as he put it, was full — the inspiration of the Mississippi was still with him from the previous summer — and creativity drove him like a demon. On August 22 he wrote to Howells: "I have written eight or nine hundred manuscript pages in such a brief space of time that I mustn't name the number of days; I shouldn't believe it myself . . .[130]

Selections from the new story appeared in the *Century* for December, 1883, January, 1884, and February, 1884. In February the book was announced for publication. By the spring of 1884 Charles Webster, manager of Twain's own publishing house, had the book well in hand; and in April, Twain was worrying about having to read proof. Then the book was withheld from publication while subscription sales mounted. It appeared at last in England on December 4 and in the United States in February, 1885.

Neither Cable nor Clemens specifies what "deep subjects" they talked about during 1881-83 — the true gestation period for *Huckleberry Finn*. We know that they talked about such things as books, writers, lecturing, politics, and religion. When Cable was convalescing in Twain's home the talk of the two men was, Cable wrote, "generally earnest — about our great Century & the vast advantages of living in it . . . ."[131] It is inevitable that they should have talked much of southern people and the southern ethos. Class and caste, ethics according to regional ritual, and ethics according to "the Higher Law" were, from 1882 through 1885, topics uppermost in the mind of Cable; and society in the Mississippi Valley was, for at least part of this time, uppermost in the mind of Clemens. That part of Cable's views that Twain did not get directly in conversation he got from his fiction. Twain knew few intellectuals or artists at all intimately, and Cable may well have been the first southerner he had ever known who, like himself, had become emancipated from major regional prejudices and was prepared to examine southern customs and the southern social structure from a "liberal" point of view.[132] Like any liberal Cable is open to attack by conservatives for believing too firmly in natural rights and for failing to take prescriptive rights seriously enough, for overestimating the importance of logic and for underestimating the importance of custom. But Cable was intelligently liberal. In his short stories and early novels he tried to portray Negroes as having naturally the complement of virtues and vices normal to all men; and he was shrewd enough to show, also, how they differed from other men by reason of environmental pressures. Twain must have noted the temerity with which Cable handled dramatic — sometimes melodramatic — situations involving miscegenation and romantic love between the races.

There can be no doubt that when Cable talked with Twain of civil rights in the New South he expounded the views — fundamentally views on the need for justice in human relations — that he set out in *The Silent South* (1885) and in *The Negro Question* (1888). These views were provocative in the North; in the South they were judged to be hideously subversive. Just as subversive, but less obviously so, was the notable passage in *Huck Finn* in which Huck invents the blowing of a cylinder head: "Good gracious! anybody hurt?" Aunt Sally asks. "No'm. Killed a nigger," Huck answers. "Well, it's lucky," Aunt Sally says thankfully; "because sometimes people do get hurt."

Cable cannot be compared with Twain in ability to treat southern institutions and southern mores dramatically, but he deserves credit for being first to work in the field with full understanding. And Cable, the lesser artist, had the advantage of a logical mind. Although he was not a profound thinker, Twain thought he was one, and his analytical reflections on the social and moral situation of the South were entirely adequate to reinforce and complement Twain's emotional, "reconstructed" inclinations. The fact is that in *Huckleberry Finn* Twain examined southern frontier society and the culture of the Mississippi Valley with a mind deepened and enriched by reading and experience. His eyes were the gifted eyes of a loving ex-member of the culture who had become a moderately sophisticated, sharply critical world citizen. Cable was the only other prominent southern writer of the time who had effected a fusion at all similar, the only one of Twain's friends who could easily have helped Twain to precipitate and order his ideas about the South. Certainly the entire history of the association makes clear that it was a fruitful one, though in widely different senses, for both men. Quite possibly Cable gave more than did Twain, and Twain learned more than did Cable during their brief, jangled friendship.

LETTERS

Hartford, July 17/81

My Dear Mr. Cable —

The book[1] has come; I read it last night, & the charm of it, & the pain of it, & the deep music of it are still pulsing through me. I could echo Howells's strong admirations, now, if he were here. (He spent a day with me last week, & we had much pleasant talk of you & your books.) Howells is still in the mind to go to New Orleans with me in November for the Mississippi trip, & we shall hope to see you then. Maybe you could find time to visit a Creole camp with us.

With sincere thanks, I am

Truly Yours
S. L. Clemens

Hartford, June 20/82

My Dear Cable —

Confound it, the "menagerie" has to be given up for a year. Both Howells & Aldrich are to be absent a long time in Europe; & then Uncle Remus[2] vanished southward again, without giving us a chance — according to agreement — to try the strength of his voice in some empty Boston hall. I suppose that if we ever do get the menagerie on its feet we can't hope to have Remus, because he evidently can't conquer his diffidence.

Osgood[3] was here last night, & we had a pleasant talk about our trip & all you charming people. I wish you would remember me gratefully to our friends the Guthries,[4] & also to Mrs. Cox[5] and Miss Nellie.[6] (Which reminds me that I've ordered 2 copies of my new Sketches[7] to be sent to you — one of them is for Miss Nellie, with my affectionate regards.)

Our packing is all finished, today, & a special car engaged to transport our family to Elmira N. Y. for the summer — but now a horrible rash appears upon the body of the baby![8] — & there is much scarlet fever in the town. The child has been pretty sick during several days; consequently we are now all of a sudden become unspeakably alarmed. The doctor cannot tell, yet, whether this rash is only heat or the other dreadful thing.

Please remember me to Mrs. Cable, & thank her for her courtesies & kindnesses to me what time I broke the bread & ate the salt of hospitality under her roof. And if there is scarlet fever near, gather the babies to your breast & fly the town!

Sincerely Yours
S L Clemens

Cable's letter of June 29 reflects something of his circumstances and aspirations at the time. The speech at Oxford was an important milestone in his career.[9] He had given up his clerkship, was a full-time writer, and was dreaming of the possibility of paid public appearances. Moreover, he was setting in order his ideas on society in the South, particularly with respect to the Negro. Although he did not treat the Negro question directly in this address, he did make at this time his first formal, nonfictional approach to the ills of the South as he saw them.

His letter is misleading in important particulars. In the first place, his voice did not carry well beyond the first few rows. Second, he stirred resentment by charging the South with being regrettably outside the main current of American thought, and although his tone seems to have been conciliatory, his ideas met strong disapproval. Indeed, it is said that inattention grew at one point into a disorder that led General Stewart, Chancellor of the University, to request attention from the audience. It is likewise reported that the Reverend C. K. Marshall, who had preached the commencement sermon, rose in ire at the conclusion of Cable's address, censured him for unpatriotic utterances, and charged the young people not to forget the principles for which their fathers had fought. The students applauded Marshall vigorously.

That Cable glossed over the adverse reception accorded this address did not mean that he intended to give up his principles or a possible career as a speaker. He was quietly stubborn, and it may be that the hostility of his audience confirmed him in those liberal principles which he championed boldly and logically from this time on. Nor did deficiency of voice make him give up lecturing as a possible source of income. Instead, for the next few years he worked hard, privately and with teachers of "elocution," to improve his volume and delivery.

New Orleans, June 29th, 1882

Dear Mr. Clemens:

Your letter of 20th keeps me anxious. *Is* it scarlet fever or is it prickly heat.[10] The white elephant was rec'd by us through the mail — many thanks. I took it with me on the cars on my way to Oxford, Miss. day before yesterday and read it with laughter and prolonged applause.[11]

I think I told you I had promised to make the annual oration there to the University of Miss. It's done & I still live. I had a chance to try my voice & platform courage. I am said to have scored a decided success. The house was full — crowded except in the gallery — & probably contained 800 people. I spoke for an hour & three quarters with frequent interruptions of applause to the end. Only under the low badly constructed galleries at the far end of the room was I not heard, though I made no special effort.

So I am the more regretful that the menagerie has to be given up.

Mrs. Cable & all the ladies of my two households send kindest wishes & hopes that you are not to have sickness among your children.

Please remember me to Mrs. Clemens & oblige,
Yours truly,
G. W. Cable

New York, Sep. 26, 1882

My dear Mr. Clemens:

Here I am. Just before I left home my conscience overcame me, my talent for delay lost its usual vigor & I got Mrs. Cable to promise me that the picture of the old black nurse, which my sister[12] did for you soon after you left us, should go to you by express.

The copy is not as well done as I wished, & I hoped my sister would find time to make a better, which she also wished to do; but she was not well & getting behind with her work, saw no early opportunity of repeating the copy.

Mrs. Cable has used, in packing it, a castaway stretcher with a rejected half finished crayon portrait on it — which please put into the fire & oblige my sister.

I am going to be two or three weeks in New York & hope to run up & see you for a day if you will let me.

May I? & when in October. About the middle? Will you be at home? Say for one day?

My warmest regards to Mrs. Clemens.

Yours truly,
G. W. Cable

New York, Friday 3.15 PM [Sept. 29, 1882?]

My Dear Cable —

I've rushed in here,[13] with 30 minutes to spare before rushing for the Hartford train — but I've missed you. Arrived yesterday evening with my whole tribe & 2 cats, from the summer vacation. Shall reach Hartford this evening. A week hence, we shall be all straightened up, there; & then we shall be glad & willing & anxious to see you on any date thereafter — you to name it & give us notice & we will go to your train & fetch you. Be *sure* you come.

I must rush now, or I shan't get my tribe ready for the train.

Sincerely Yours
S L Clemens

Hartford Conn. Oct. 5th.1882.

My Dear Cable,

Did you get my note written in the Century office? I want you to choose your own date and come; we are ready for you now any time. Give us several days if you can without detriment to your work. Change of scene and people may be even a help to your work. If you can stay the longer by coming now, come now; but if you can stay the longer by coming later, come later.

Yours sincerely,
S. L. Clemens

84

NYork, Oct. 9, 1882

D'r Mr Clemens.[14]

I got your note written at the Century office. I am anxious to see you, but do not know exactly when I can come to you. It must be a flying trip when I make it; a day or two at most.

Mrs. Cable writes me that for good reasons she delayed sending the picture of the "mammy" but *now* it must be on the way, if it has not reached you already.

Many thanks for your kind invitation to prolong my stay.

Yours truly
G. W. Cable

Hartford Conn. Oct. 12th. 1882

My Dear Cable,

The portrait has arrived, and repeats the original to a perfection that is astonishing. It seems to me that the work on it is even finer than that on the original if possible.

There is but one picture in the house that is equally satisfactory. There are two or three excellent pictures in the house, but none that I could not manage to get along without, at a pinch, except this one other. But I will tell you all about it when you come, and you may judge the portrait for yourself. I have forgotten what I was to be alowed [*sic*] to pay for it, but was confidently expecting Osgood to be able to tell me, but his memory proves as treacherous as mine; says he cannot call the sum to mind. I ought to be ashamed, but I never remember anything whatever except humiliation. If by some lucky chance there had been humiliation mixed in, I could remember every detail of that day for a thousand years. You must help me with your memory now, and I will hold myself under obligation to you forever. Meantime I beg you to tell Mrs. Cox how delighted we all are with her work, but don't let her find out that I have forgotten anything. With you to help me I can get that matter straight.

Warner[15] is home now, Twichell[16] is home, we are all at home; and are hoping you will come up as soon as you can.

Sincerely Yours,
S. L. Clemens

N. York Oct 14, 1882

My dear Mr. Clemens:

Go to sleep. Go to sleep. The reason you forget what you was to pay for the "mammy" is that you was not to pay anything. It was to be indicative of my desire to make you remember that you once walked up & down my little workshop with Osgood sitting here & me there and Mrs. Cable yonder, and Uncle Remus on the other side; & that fellowship filled the place from floor to ceiling & from the window that looked out into the orange tree, to the door that stood open on the balcony.

You promised to do me the favor to accept mammy.

Did I ever tell you her name? It's as good as the picture. It's

Madame Maptiste.

I hope to be in Hartford in a week or ten days, but will telegraph you.

Kind regards to Mrs. Clemens, Mr. Warner & all — each by name, please.

Yours truly
G. W. Cable

Hartford Conn. Oct. 16th. 1882.

My Dear Cable,

All right, to sleep I go; until I get you here and put you under the cross-question, —— possibly to the torture. Meantime, I shall hope that you will reach here as soon as you are expecting to do so. I have been collecting some beautiful weather, and a comet and a lot of other things which Mrs. Clemens and I supposed might please you, to show what we can do up North when we try. And besides, I shall finish my book[17] this week I think, for I have already just finished writing all I don't know about New Orleans.

Truly Yours,
S. L. Clemens.

Cable made visits to Boston and Hartford in the autumn of 1882.[18] His reputation had preceded him, and he was cordially received everywhere that he went in the North. From about this time literary and academic circles were especially hospitable. After speaking at the University of Mississippi in June, 1882, he went on to Washington and Lee to receive an honorary Doctor of Letters. In the spring of 1883 he addressed the "Academical Department" of the University of Louisiana, and Yale University presented him with an honorary Master of Arts. In the following letter he refers to his visit to Hartford.

New Orleans, Nov. 7, 1882

Dear Mr. Clemens:

I'm not going to try to say anything—adequate. I am here to thank you and Mrs. Clemens for your delightful hospitality, but what shall I say. I kiss my hand. I kiss Mrs. Clemens hand. I get out my handkerchief. But all is ineffectual—insufficient. Embrace the dear little girls, Susie, Clara & Jean for me. My children listen to my accounts of them, & of your home, with sparkling eyes.

I sent the books to you a day or two ago, (on the 4th). Mrs. Cable had failed to find them all and even now they do not conform exactly to the list you kept.

I would thank you to remember me cordially to the Warners[19] & Twitchells [sic], Dr. Parker,[20] & Messrs. Cheeney[21] & Dunham[22]—& Genl. Hawley[23]—& the Monday Club generally.[24]

All here send love.

Yours truly
G. W. Cable

Hartford, Nov. 11th. 1882.

My Dear Cable;-

The books all came, and I am infinitely obliged. I have only time for a note to say this and add the hope that you reached home safe and well, and found all your relatives and friends comfortable.

The old mammie is nicely framed and makes a most effective addition to the library wall.

With kindest regards to yourself and wife and both of the families, I am

Sincerely yours,

S. L. Clemens

P. S.   Please send me a New Orleans directory of this or last year. I do not know the price but inclose five dollars at random.

S. L. C.

Writing a post card to Clemens on January 9, Cable referred to a "speech" that he delivered on the night of January 8. Perhaps he used the word "speech" to suggest that he was continuing to train himself for the public platform. What he actually gave was a detailed, impressive report in his capacity as secretary of the Prisons and Asylums Aid Association. The first annual meeting of this association, held at Grunewald Hall, was fully covered in the *Times-Democrat,* which had supported the association, for January 9. Two-and-one-half columns of a story that ran to more than five columns were devoted to Cable's report. Less space was given to the remarks of the president, W. R. Lyman, and to the "main address" by the Reverend Hugh Miller Thompson.

In his report Cable summarized the results of the first year's work of the association and stressed the achievement of the association in bringing about the abolition of a parish asylum in New Orleans and in having its inmates transferred to better quarters at Jackson, Louisiana. The greater part of his paper was devoted, however, to an account of the continuing barbarities permitted in Louisiana, particularly in the New Orleans parish prison.

Undoubtedly the zeal Cable displayed in urging the reform of asylums and prisons increased the resentment that many conservative Louisianians were beginning to feel for him. The *Times-Democrat,* a "progressive" paper, had made a considerable financial contribution to the work of the association; but *L'Abeille,* organ of the Creoles, neglected to report the meeting.

Materials gathered while investigating the prisons went into *Dr. Sevier,* not very skillfully integrated, and helped fan resentment against Cable when that book appeared in September, 1884.

New Orleans, Jan 9, 1883.

My Dear Uncle;[25]

Have you, among the books I sent you, a second volume of a work by a man named Stuart? The fellow I stole it from is on the track of it and our state hotels are so incommodious that I prefer to have the book on hand when called for. If you are not done with it, keep it a few days longer—and the others as long as you please.—Made a speech last night—50 minutes—audience made no complaint.

Love to all
Yours,
G. W. C.[26]

Hartford Jan 15/83

My Dear Nephew—

I have just finished my book[27] at last, & was about to return the volumes you so kindly lent me. I'll get'm started this afternoon or tomorrow. I am a little short-handed, in the Executive department, the coachman's family being down with scarlet fever—so I find myself a trifle overloaded with jobs which I don't know the hang of. Two of our children are pretty sick, too—& 2½ weeks ago my secretary went home with scarlet fever, & since then I have disposed of 120 letters, January bills, & so on. My life is a trifle too busy these days.

Sincerely Yours
S L Clemens

When an audience do not complain, it is a compliment, & when they *do* it is a compliment, too, if unaccompanied by violence.[28]

N.O. Jan 18, 1883

Never mind the book. I have it. I found it last night where I have found a great many books—to wit, in my bookcase. Pardon me for troubling you. Mrs. C. sends love. Love to all yours.

Yours truly
G. W. Cable[29]

Roswell Smith, editor of the *Century Magazine,* Cable's outlet for stories and articles, offered advice, aid, and encouragement when Cable began his career as a professional man of letters.[30] Clemens, too, lent a helping hand. Clemens had in mind, first, a tour to be made by five or six distinguished performers, and, when that project fell through, a joint lecture tour. Like Smith, he urged Cable to try the platform.

Accompanied by Richard Watson Gilder, Cable visited the Johns Hopkins University in October, 1882. President Daniel C. Gilman commissioned the novelist to prepare eight lectures on "The Relations of Literature to Modern Society" to be delivered the following March. Cable actually prepared and delivered five lectures in Hopkins Hall, beginning on March 5 and ending on March 16. The response of press and public was so enthusiastic that Gilman requested Cable to give a reading. This reading, given on March 19, was in turn so popular that on March 22 Cable offered two more.

After a brief stay in New York, Cable made a public appearance on April 4 in Hartford. Two private readings and a variety of social engagements followed. His audiences were enchanted, and he was elated. Twain, Smith, and others puffed his swelling sails. Charles Dudley Warner contributed a letter to the *Century* for June praising his readings, especially those before small audiences.

Hartford Mch 7/83

My Dear Cable:

Roswell Smith has sent us your letter. Now to business. Warner[31] & I had a talk last night. Our idea is thus; That we secure a nice little hall here—Unity Hall—& trot you out before an appreciative little audience—not for pecuniary profit for you, & yet not at any *expense* to you—but simply for the attainment of *these* important objects, viz:

1.   That you may try your lecture;

2.   That you may try your lecture-wings;

3.   That you may have the right sort of newspaper attention; and

4.   That the total results shall be a valuable advertisement.

If you coincide, all right. We then proceed to the next division of the business—to wit:

1.   Title of the lecture;

2.   Date.

"Creole Women" is *good.*

If that is it—or *whatever* the title may be—drop us a line & let us know, right away.

Give us a date—not *short* of 2 weeks hence—& put *that* in your letter. Give us a day or two's leeway or choice on one or both sides of the date you name, as the hall might happen to be already engaged for the date you especially name.

Then Warner & I will sail in!

Sincerely yours,
S L Clemens

Keep Roswell Smith posted.

Hartford Saturday [March 17, 1883]

My Dear Cable—

You are to lecture here the 3d of April, on "Creole Women", in Unity Hall. So *that's* all arranged. Formal invitation, duly signed by prominent citizens, will be presently sent you.[32] Advertising will shortly begin.[33] Preliminary "paragraphing" will begin NOW. Stir up Roswell Smith, please, & have him gather his clan & make preparation.

Now to *other* business. This morning, while I was getting out of bed, an idea struck me; & when I had finished putting on my socks it was already in a state of completion, & I said "Now I'll write to Cable & say, *don't make any more lecture engagements till we've had a talk.*" That is what I *do* say. What you *have* made, *fill,* but don't make any more till you've seen me.

Yrs Ever
Mark.

Balto. Mch 20, 1883

Dear Uncle Mark:

This community is trying to waltz me off my feet or else I would have somewhere & somehow a chance to write you a genteel letter.

I have yours of Saturday & one earlier, kindly inviting me, in Mrs. Clemens name as well as your own, to sojourn within the borders of your tabernacle. Many thanks. Mr. & Mrs.

George Warner, however, have rented me & taken the bill down, lo, these many days.

I shall make no engagements until I hear from—I mean until I see you. I gave yesterday afternoon my initial *reading* in Hopkins Hall. Subject "Creole dialects". The hall was simply cramfull & the audience in almost continual laughter. It's touchingly gratifying to hear them laugh & applaud where nothing funny is intended.

Good bye—man waiting to drive me out to the insane asylum. Tries to keep me gentle by telling me he's going to bring me back.

Yours truly
G. W. Cable

Love to the household.

Hartford, March 23d, 1883.

My Dear Nephew:

Mrs. Clemens and I got home from New York last night, where we had been since Monday morning. Warner dropped in and the suggestion was made that in view of the high success of your reading, in Baltimore, you deliver the same reading here instead of the proposed lecture.[34] The idea is exceedingly sound. This occasion being an advertisement, an untried lecture is not the safest thing. The safest thing is a reading which has been tried and has succeeded. We move that you do the reading instead of the lecture. The lecture will come good after you shall have made your reputation. Also, we want to change your date and make it one day later, that is to say the fourth of April if that will be convenient for you. The reason is Warner cannot be here on the fourth but can be here on the third [*sic*]. Let me know by telegram about these several things; give me your decision, and whatever it may be it shall be respected. I sent all this by telegraph to Baltimore this morning before I opened your letter. I did not open any letters at the usual hour, because we are in a good deal of a flurry here. One of the coachman's children is dying and since midnight Mrs. Clemens has been rather alarmingly ill.

Yours in haste & c.
S. L. Clemens.

92

For Cable the friendly atmosphere at Hartford and the praise that he received following his three readings proved a heady tonic, something very different from the hostility he had left behind him in New Orleans. On April 7 he addressed an expansive letter to his "precious Mother," writing while on the train between Hartford and Newport, "running down along the edge of the river in the beautiful Connecticut Valley."[35] Optimism over the future made him even more joyously sensitive than usual to the charms of the landscape, which he described in fulsome detail: great hills rise brown and grey; white foaming torrents tumble down mossy rocks; land soaked by falling rain has withal a look of spring promise.

There was promise of spring for the Cables, too:

My visit to Hartford has been full of pleasure & profit. A new future appears to be opening before me. To *us* the brown winter of the past seems just ready to give birth to a green & roseate spring, and if it be so I rejoice that you have been spared to share it . . .

I scored another emphatic success last evening in a reading before a small drawing-room audience of 55 persons at Mr Warner's house. Charles Dudley Warner was delighted with it. He kept away from me until I had heard all the adulation of the 55, & when all the house was abed but he & I, said "now let's come down to business." The only criticism he had was a warning to speak loud & slow enough when I get into a large hall. All the rest was a discussion of my literary method, which he puts above all other American fictionists.

In this same letter Cable informs his mother that he left Hartford without being able to see Mrs. Clemens, who was slowly and "tedeously" improving. Twain answers what must have been a solicitous inquiry in his next letter.

Hartford, April 16th. 1883

My Dear Cable:—

There is not much to say about Mrs. Clemenses case. I am not sure that she is any further ahead than she was when you were here. She has no disease, now, but then she has no appetite. Consequently she gains no strength, but stands still; that is, lies still, mainly. However, as soon as she shall be able to travel on a mattress, I shall take her to Elmira, N. Y., and see if her mother can nurse her back to health.

I hope you will require money in advance. Mere written guaranty of those thieves is worth nothing. They will leave a loop-hole in the writing through which their small souls can creep.

I shall be at the authors club[36] and the Salvini[37] banquet in case Mrs. Clemens is well enough to spare me—a doubtful outlook. Mrs. Clemens and I send warmest regards to you and Mrs. Cable.

Yours Sincerely

S. L. Clemens

New Orleans, May 22, 1883

Dear Uncle Mark:

I have just telegraphed my inability to attend the Sat'y M'g Club[38] reunion. It would be a long walk in the hot sun and like as not I'd get there too late after all. If I attempted to ride the conductor would probably catch me and somebody would tell my mother. I decided I'd better not try to come.

The invitation did not arrive in time for me to answer by letter.

Yesterday afternoon we received your two copies (1 for 'cross 'street)[39] of Life on the Mississippi. The family are devouring it—not goat fashion exactly, but next thing to it. It got hold of me this morning and the result is this letter will probably miss one mail.

All send love. None too young & none too old to do that here. Thank you for conveying the young ladies' invitation. Why *didn't* you say how Mrs. Clemens is.

Love to all.—Stop!

I have a letter from one Sidney Drake[40] of your town, proposing for me to write a successful book for him to publish. His anxiety to make me rich overwhelms me with gratitude. Whenever you're writing—for there's no need of making the matter the main subject of a letter—tell me what you know about it. No hurry.

Love to all.

Yours truly,

G. W. Cable

As a preliminary to writing his letter of June 4 in answer to Cable's letter of May 22, Clemens made notes across the face of Cable's letter: "Was in Canda [*sic*] when this came. Girls were delighted Good [written across the lines in which Cable told of devouring Twain's *Life on the Mississippi,* almost goat-fashion]. Mrs. C. improving Don't know Drake Love to you all."

94

My Dear Cable:

The girls were mightily delighted with your telegram. I am ever so glad you sent it. They had a royal time at their reception, but I missed it through being at a social spree in Canada.[41] This reminds me that I think I have acquired a Canadian copyright[42] at last. We have gone at it ignorantly and wrong-end first, heretofore. But this time I believe we have made no mistakes. We have done everything plainly, and squarely, have evaded no laws, wronged nobody, and yet I think our Canadian copyright is as good and strong as our English one.

I do not know Sidney Drake. That is nothing against his fame, because there are celebrated business men in Hartford whom I never have heard of. I merely have not happened to hear of this one; therefore I do not know how he stands as a publisher. But there is one thing which I do know; and that is, that if I were going to advise you to issue through a Hartford house, I would say, every time, go to my former publishers, The American Publishing Company, 284 Asylum St. They swindled me out of huge sums of money in the old days, but they do know how to push a book; and besides, I think they are honest people now. I think there was only one thief in the concern, and he is shoveling brimstone now.[43]

Mrs. Clemens is steadily improving, and probably weighs thirty or forty pounds now. We leave here for the summer a couple of weeks hence,[44] and then I shall expect her to come right up and be her old self within thirty days. We all send love and best wishes to you all.

Truly Yours,
S. L. Clemens

During the spring and summer of 1883 Cable was in New York much of the time, training his voice, completing *Dr. Sevier,* and giving a few readings. After much serious thought and following consultations with three clergymen, he went to his first play. He expanded in the company of wealthy, cultivated, and friendly men and women. That autumn he gave a set of important readings in Boston, his introduction being taken care of by

Howells, Thomas Bailey Aldrich, E. P. Whipple, John Boyle O'Reilly, and Oliver Wendell Holmes, who signed a "card" that appeared in the Boston newspapers:

We hope that the readers of Mr. George W. Cable's sketches and romances of Creole life are all aware that he is soon to give in Boston three of the readings from his own books, which have elsewhere so admirably interpreted his characterizations. In asking general attention to the fact, we feel that we are doing a favor to every one who has appreciated the peculiar and delicate charm of Mr. Cable's work.[45]

Edwin Booth sat with Aldrich in Boston's Chickering Hall at the first reading on November 26. Howells, too, heard Cable and had most of literary and social Boston to a reception in his honor. A flattering advance notice for this reading appeared in the *Post* on the twenty-sixth, and notices and comments appeared regularly in this and other papers. The *Morning Journal*[46] reviewed his second and third scheduled readings, the third attracting particular attention because of the inclusion of Creole and Negro songs and chants:

Almost every phase of the local melodies was rendered, from the barbaric plaint of the boatman to the touching chant of one who mourned the fact that the affections of him she loved had been stolen from her. Mr. Cable, nowithstanding his deprecating musical criticism, sang with a purity of tone and intelligent phrasing that won the favor of the audience in a marked degree. The songs of the smugglers, the runaway slaves and the various accompaniments to the primitive dances were given with much spirit. . . .

The three scheduled readings were so successful (Chickering Hall seated 460 and was full or nearly full for each reading) that Cable added a "farewell" matinee performance for December 11. This, too, was favorably reviewed,[47] and Cable gave one more matinee, this one at "Chickering's Piano Rooms" on December 14.

There is no doubt that Boston approved of Cable. The *Transcript* printed his entire address given on December 6 before the XIX Century Club in New York.[48] After this, he was in and out of New York giving readings until January 27. On that day he had the misfortune to fall ill in Hartford, of what is variously said to have been influenza, facial neuralgia, measles, or mumps, during what was to have been a short visit to the Clemenses. It has been suggested that this visit, assisted by Cable's April Fool joke, cemented the friendship between the two writers.[49] Actually, it is much more likely that the prolonged visit acted as an abrasive and brought about the first break in what had promised to be a harmonious friendship.[50] Mark and Livy had entirely too many sick friends on their hands at one time or another, and Livy was never very well herself.

96

In addition to growing weary of having Cable around, Mark, who generally held himself or God to be directly responsible for all family misfortunes, thought bitterly that Cable passed mumps on to Clara, Jean, and Susy. That Cable's physician was positive that Cable did not have mumps made no difference to Mark.[51] He wrote to Howells:

... Susie's turn. She has had 4 of the most hellfiredest days & nights, now, with the mumps — has suffered 13 times more than Cable did (whose pains lasted but 2 days), & yet has not made as much fuss in the 4 days as he used to make in 15 minutes; though she has shed whole barrels of noiseless tears.[52]

The antipathy towards Cable that he developed at this time remained strong six months later. He wrote, in what connection is not clear:

... I notice that Mrs. Howells mentions Cable. Privately — she mustn't do anything on *our* account. I venture this impertinence with misgivings that I am taking too much of a liberty; & if this instinct is unhappily correct, I hope she will forgive, & forget that I said anything. My only excuse is that I thought — well, dam it you know what I thought.[53]

With Joseph Pennell, the artist, in charge of local arrangements, Cable was scheduled to read in Association Hall at Philadelphia on Monday, January 28, and again on the afternoon of Saturday, February 2.[54] The newspapers in Philadelphia noted the progress of his illness and reviewed his readings, when he finally gave them on February 19, 22, and 24.[55]

The story of Cable's illness as told by the following letters from Mrs. Clemens, Mrs. George Warner, and Clemens may be supplemented by referring to four letters that Cable wrote or dictated on January 28, 30, 31, and February 13.[56]

Feb. 1st. 84

Dear Mrs Cable

Mr Cable has been sleeping so much today that I have not found a time when he was awake long enough to dictate to you—but if you could see how bright he is today, it would delight your heart and put it at rest, I am sure. He was restless last night, he says there was no cause for it except that he kept thinking. My judgment is that perhaps he slept rather too much yesterday to be able to sleep last night. However he is much better today, has eaten two good meals & is soon to have an other. When he has been awake he has been watching in the trees for a squirrell & at last he found one & called me to see it.

I hope you will have no undue anxiety, knowing that we will let you know just how he is from day to day.

I think it more than likely that he will be dressed tomorrow.

With sincere sympathy yours
Olivia L. Clemens

Hartford. Saturday. Feb. 2d 1884.

My dear Mrs. Cable,

Yesterday afternoon, — to go on with the story — Mr. Cable sat up quite a while, seemed very bright & chatty, saw his agent, Mr. Pond, with whom he had a very satisfactory business talk, and seemd much better after the visit. But later the pain in his head returned and he had a restless night with considerable fever. This morning, altho' he is tired from such a night, the doctor finds him in better general condition — better tongue, & on the whole improved.

He seems cheerful this morning. It seems to be intermittent. The doctor has been giving Quinine all along, but today will give it in a different form that he thinks may be more digestible & act more quickly.

For breakfast he had oat meal and for his second meal will eat beef-steak and tapioca & jelly — & will probably eat one other hearty meal before night. He really seems to relish his food, & particularly his beef steak yesterday & his oat meal this morning.

Mrs. Clemens is a great believer in plenty of nourishment in such cases, and so, tho' he feels quite weak, his strength cannot get very low. He walks to the bath-room and really has considerable strength, though he doesn't incline to sit up very much. You surely need not feel anxious, dear Mrs. Cable, but we all feel how trying it must be to you to have him ill away from you. It is one of those, slow, trying things that needs patience more than anything else.

98

If there is any cause for anxiety be assured that you will be kept informed. But we expect nothing of the sort. I am writing for Mrs. Clemens who is occupied just now.

Very sincerely yours
L. G. Warner.[57]
Hartford, Feb. 3/84

My Dear Pond—

He is in no danger, but I do not believe he will be out of bed for several weeks, yet. I am sure he will not stand on a platform again this season.

Now that you have read this, please send it to Gilder; for it contains the news & will save me a letter — I've got a lot of others to write, to friends who wish to hear.

I will drop you a line every few days; oftener, if anything of importance to report.

Truly Yours
S. L. Clemens

Be sure & send it to Gilder.

Hartford Feb. 6th 1884

Dear Mrs. Cable

I am going to send you only a line today & take some of your letter time to write Mr Cable's mother.

Mr. Cable is still better than yesterday, slept all night last night, sat up yesterday & today. Eats with appetite and I think will very soon be himself again.

Hoping that you have rec'd the letters regularly

I am very truly yours

Olivia L. Clemens

Thursday Feb. 7th .84

Dear Mrs Cable

I congratulate you Mr Cable is up today and dressed. I have been conselling [sic] him not to stay up too long but to go back to bed & get up often. He eats well and seems like himself.

I think by tomorrow or next day he will come out to his meals — at least to one of them.

99

So I think now it will not be necessary for me to send you any more messages, alone that is. Mr. Cable will undoubtedly write you himself by day after tomorrow. We think him now quite a well man.

Very sincerely yours
Olivia L Clemens

Major Pond may have had occasion to regret the invitation that he extended to Mark in the following letter. Twain had a passion for firing off inquiries, instructions, and complaints to anyone who would assist him with business or domestic problems, and he had hundreds of them.

New York, Feb. 16 1884

My dear Mr. Clemens:

The young man arrived all right yesterday. I met him at the Depot. The journey seemed to do him good. He ate a tremendous dinner — I wonder if you have been starving him all the time? — I think I never saw a more wholesome feedi[n]g. He is again at it this morning. He & Cary have gone out to buy an overcoat, & things. I feel quite in hopes that his normal appetite will return. If it does not he will have to get some hotel victim that runs his house on the American plan. He recommends me if I must be sick to be sure & go to your house, & to have his nurse: all of which I have under consideration. He seems very full of thankfulness, & his principal conversation is good things about you & your household.

I will once more express my gratitude in my weak way, for the good you have done Mr. Cable, (my friend means *me*) when I can run of [*sic*] any errands for you here & you fail to draw on me, I shall withdraw in proportion to the enormity of the offense, a certain amount of my love.

Yours very truly
J. B. Pond
(over)

Dear, dear Mark & dear Mrs. Clemens:

Pond was just closing this letter when I came in, & lets me add a P.S.

God bless you! May something, — *anything* that isn't afflic-

100

tion or distress — cure you of swearing & so make you *perfect-ly* lovely!

Blessed be your hall & your board; blessed be your guest chamber, your larder & your cellar & angels attend you, your sweet wife & your lovely children. May I trouble you to let me hear how Clara & Jean are.

Yours ever
G. W. Cable

Feb 18, 1884.

Dear Friend:

I have some concern to know what has become of Ambulinia.[58] Did you give it to Dr. Bacon,[59] or shall I look for it more diligently among my effects. I can't find it anywhere. I'm afraid I'm troubling for nothing — unnecessarily, I mean, — & hope you will pardon me.

Yours truly
G. W. Cable

Philadelphia Feb. 21, 1884.

Dear Mark Twain:

Well!

Haven't I been a troublesome customer!

But I've found Ambulinia; love is triumphant, and Pond has expressed my dress suit from N.York. I'll get it early tomorrow morning.

If I can pick up any other mild contagion about the country anywhere I'll bring it to your house, you seem so pleased to have me give your babies the mumps.[60]

Well, never mind; if you ever get the whooping-cough, come and see us down in New Orleans; Mrs. Cable will be delighted to see you.

There's one comfort — the new diagnosis relieves me from all the blame for my thin overcoat. Checkmate!

Good night. I've no business to be up writing letters. Love to all — the Warners,[61] too.

Yours truly,
G. W. CABLE

Reporters, critics, Ozias Pond, Major Pond, old friends and stray acquaintances, all thought of Twain as "the great humorist." Cable was "the New Orleans novelist," the "painter of Creole life." Moralists sometimes charged that Twain's language and situations were in dubious taste. An eccentric minority—which Twain's admirers might have taken to be composed mainly of fretful aesthetes and hypersophisticated Bostonians and Frenchmen—held that Twain's humor was, very often, feeble, crude, and painfully worked up. Almost no one except Howells, West or East, saw that Twain was a great sentimental, realistic novelist with a humorous vein that could be shallow or tiresome but which was sometimes extraordinarily good when subordinated to larger purposes.

Although Cable generally curbed his own more extravagantly humorous impulses and although he lacked both Twain's vitality and his remarkable ability to add verbal salt to a comic situation, his sense of humor was perhaps basically not unlike that with which Twain could at will delight his admirers. In Philadelphia, after he had been ill at the home of the Clemenses in Hartford, Cable played an impromptu physical prank on his friend Joseph Pennell. When Pennell called on him at his hotel, Cable had Major Pond let his friend into the bedroom after he had jumped into bed, clothes and all. Cable lay with the whites of his eyes turned up, his mouth open, gasping and softly moaning until the distressed Pennell took his hand and began a consoling speech. Then Cable burst with laughter.

Newspapers, biographers, and literary historians have given absurdly pleased, disproportionate attention to the April Fool joke that Cable concocted for the delectation of Twain, a joke founded on Twain's hatred for autograph seekers. Cable sent out nearly two hundred letters to Twain's friends urging them to write for his autograph, timing their requests so that they would reach him on April 1. Cable's own letter seems flat, but some letters were mildly amusing. Dean Sage, remembering Twain's poisonous hostility towards Bret Harte, requested his autograph for a young lady who considered Clemens' "The Heathen Chinee" a delightful poem.[62]

Cable's April Fool letter to Twain was addressed from Chicago. After recovering from his illness, he had read to enthusiastic hearers in Philadelphia and in the Middle West. At Ann Arbor his name was posted in two-foot letters and a brass band tooted for dear life to get an audience together.[63] In Chicago he gave readings every day for a week in Hershey Music Hall, on Madison Street near Dearborn, appearing March 24 through March 29, and giving both matinee and evening performances on March 26.[64] Each evening he changed selections and sang two or three "Creole African" songs. Pond advertised him as fresh from triumphs in Boston and New York. Enemies in New Orleans must have frothed if they heard of the reception accorded his Creole songs and stories; one Chicago critic opined that he gave "a thoroughly sympathetic word picture of Creole life."[65]

Chicago, Mch. 29. 1884.

Mr. Mark Twain:

I have been a devoted admirer of your works for the last sixty years. My life has been worth living ever since you began to write. Should you ever cease writing I should commit suicide on receiving the intelligence. Let me assure you, however, that I do not say these things to play upon your vanity. I do not believe you have any. No man who has the least spark of vanity could write your books.

I implore you for your autograph. Do not, I beseech you, refuse my request. I have, already, 9,999. I wan't one more. Just one, dear, gentle, blessed St. Mark! This will reach you on the 1st of April. I shall expect an answer by the 3rd.

Yours passionately,
G. W. CABLE

N.B. Every fellow furnish his own stamps.

New York, Apl. 15, 1884

Dear Saint Mark:

I have submitted our project of one story five times told by 5 authors, to Roswell Smith & Gilder & they are charmed with the scheme & have taken it up.[66] Don't let it out. You will hear from them. I passed through Hartford yesterday, and longed to stop — Knowing how badly you want to see me.

Love to all,

Yours truly,
G. W. Cable

After Twain and Cable signed a contract for the joint tour in July, 1884, Pond began to arrange for lecture engagements, and the two readers started working up a program. Cable and Pond may have had trouble persuading Twain to devote attention to the matter. That summer and fall he was struggling with the publishing business, confiding philosophical speculations to his notebook, and spending time and energy on the Blaine-Cleveland contest for the Presidency. It was not until September 20 that Clemens wrote from Elmira to "Charley" Webster ordering an unbound copy of *Huck Finn* to be shipped to Hartford for his use in selecting readings.[67] In October Cable assisted by going through proof sheets of *Huck Finn* in order to recommend appropriate passages.

Simsbury, Conn. Sep 10, 1884.

Dear Mark Twain:

I leave here today for Saratoga. Tomorrow I read there a composition. Next day I return to Simsbury and am ready to take up our business. We ought to meet & lay off our work, ought we not? Will you be home by & by? I have not forgotten that you have said you and Mrs. C. will come and see us here. We shall greet you with a hurrah. I hope you will come very soon. Mrs. Cable sends regards and repeats these expressions.

Yours truly
G.W.Cable

P.S. Bring 2 Gal's Humor. No pathos — I have the Pathos here. G.W.C.

My aged but respected Uncle:

I am delighted with the proof sheets[68] I have read, & got so absorbed in them that I forgot to note what pages seemed to offer best opportunity for reading; but one passage I know would be great. I mentioned it to Gilder; he thinks so, too. It is the runaway Jim's account of his investments winding up with the 10 cents "give to de po'".

I'll try to pick out some others.

Love to your family and my hottest regards to yourself.

Yours truly
G. W. CABLE

Oct. 13, 1884

Simsbury, Conn. Oct. 25, 1884

Dear Friend:

Pond and I have talked and thought much over the programme. Enclosed please find the embodiment of our conclusions. We both think that more alternation than this would weaken and *break* the effect. The time here comprised is the same as originally decided on — 2 hours. My memoranda make it so on the margin. The first and second numbers suffice to give the audience a sense that both stars are "present or accounted for" and the 3d and 4th give each a fair swing at their attention & interest without interruption.

One item in the programme shows a suggestion which I beg to offer. It is a substitute, almost literally from your text, for the phrase "Can't learn a nigger to argue." When we consider that the programme is advertised & becomes cold-blooded newspaper reading I think we should avoid any risk of appearing — even to the most thin-skinned and super-sensative [*sic*] and hypercritical matrons and misses — the faintest bit gross. In the text, whether on the printed page or in the readers utterances the phrase is absolutely without a hint of grossness; but alone on a published programme, it invites discreditable conjectures of what the context may be, from that portion of our public who cannot live without aromatic vinegar. I hope you'll pardon the liberty I take, and restore the original phrase if you think I'm entirely mistaken.

Wouldn't you say "carriages at ten"—People like to know; especially when the carriages are sleighs.

I am sending duplicate programme to Pond. Please let him have your verdict as soon as convenient. I shall be with him in N. York Monday. "King Sollermun" is enough by itself to immortalize its author. I read it privately to Waring,[69] his wife and her sister, after midnight of Thursday and I thought they would laugh themselves sick.

Love to all. Mrs. Cable seconds the motion. Carried.

Yours truly
G. W. Cable

The Mark Twain - Cable Readings.

Date etc.

1. The Music of Place Congo.
   Mr. Cable

2. Advance Sheets of "The Adventures of Huckleberry Finn.
                    [Punctuation omitted]
   a. "King Sollermun."
   b. "How come a Frenchman doan' talk like a man?"
   Mark Twain.

3. Scenes from Dr. Sevier.
   a. Narcisse, Kate Riley, Richling & Ristofalo.
                    (Browning and Courtship Scenes.)
   b. Narcisse puts on Mourning for Lady Byron.
   c. A Sound of Drums — Off for the Wars.
   d. Mary's Night Ride.
   Mr. Cable

4. Pages from_____, _____ and _____.
   a. A Ghost Story.
   b. Tragic Tale of the Fishwife.
   c. A Trying Situation.
   Mark Twain.

[Carriages at 10 o'clock.]

Twain seethed whenever Cable shied away from a nonprofit reading, as he did from reading at a meeting to sponsor international copyright and from the "Authors' Reading for the Longfellow Memorial Fund." Cable's provoking miserliness, Mark believed, made him refuse such invitations.

In a letter written on February 13, Mark advised his wife, who had made inquiry, that he would not invite Cable to lecture for nothing, that those connected with her charity must do that for themselves. Twain didn't believe that Cable "laid over" Sundays gratis, but kept an account against God. He predicted that Cable would not read without compensation in either Hartford or Heaven.[70]

Olivia Clemens followed her husband's instructions and tactfully placed before Cable an appeal for a free lecture for the benefit of the Decorative Art Society.[71]

106

My dear Mr Cable

This document has been left here and I forward it to you, thinking it may catch you in New York — and as Mr Clemens is to stay several days in Washington.

This Decorative Art Society is one of our great charities. It puts good thorough teaching at a low price, and takes some pupils without any charge or with very little if they are able to pay a little. Helping those who need to sell their productions, to make their productions worth what is paid for them.

I wish I might tell you some of the exceedingly good and worthy things that have been done by the "society" — but I will not trespass on your time to do that. I only write this note in order to give you some little idea of what the society is.

I suppose you two wanderers are truly glad that your Winter's Campaigne [sic] is ended, and that you are to have peace, at least for a little time.

I am very cordially yours

Olivia L. Clemens

March 2nd 1885

Twain's irritation at Cable's penny-pinching and formalistic piety resulted at the end of the tour in disagreeable publicity that could easily have led to a complete break between the two men.[72]

Twain and Major Pond spoke too freely before friends in New York of Cable's idiosyncrasies. Twain may have made quite a large and sourly comic story of his difficulties with the "Christ-besprinkled, psalm-singing Presbyterian."[73] A bloated, partially perverted, gossipy account of disagreements reached a New York correspondent for the *Herald* (Boston), who promptly put a news story on the wires. This story appeared in several papers on May 10.[74] According to the story, rumor told of personal conflict that extended to fisticuff among the three men. This rumor the reporter scotched as false, saying that investigation revealed only private and intangible disagreements. Cable, said the reporter, talked of hoggishness on the part of Twain in getting a disproportionate share of the glory; Twain vowed that he would never go on the platform again; and Pond complained of the charges which both of his companions entered as traveling expenses, Cable being the chief offender, charging "so highly luxurious a thing as champagne and so lowly a one as the blacking of his boots" to the partnership account. Pond, the story had it, declared the bills rendered by Cable greater curiosities of literature than the best of his Creole dialect. All three men, the reporter added, admitted that the firm of Twain, Cable, and Pond was permanently dissolved.

Twain attempted to disregard the newspaper story—it let him off lightly and his sense of guilt was probably at work—but Cable reacted with what was for him considerable vehemence.

Simsbury Ct May 15 1885

To S.L.Clemens

All intimations that you and Pond are not my Beloved Friends are false and if you can say the same of me do so as privately or as publicly as you like.

G.W. Cable[75]

Simsbury, Conn. May 16/85.

Dear Clemens:

Telegd. you last even'g & have not got reply; but without waiting to see if you are replying by letter, I write. For I see now that if you have not seen the newspaper and telegraphic slanders printed against us you will not understand, and if you have then my telegram hardly covers the main point. So I add this to assure you that all statements that I have either openly or covertly intimated anything unpleasant about you to my friends or anybody else are false from beginning to end. If you care to know it, I esteem you more highly since our winter's experience than I ever did before & should deeply regret if scandal mongers were to make an estrangement between us.

Of course I do not believe that you have said ought against me that was not intended as a friend's fair criticism among friends. Nor do I think Pond has said a word that was meant in unkindness about either of us.

I have privately called for an immediate explanation from the Boston Herald — where the thing seems to have started — & they write they have demanded as much of their New York correspondent & will report without delay.

Yours truly
G.W.Cable

108

My Dear Cable—

Your letter came yesterday evening, your telegram about noon. My dear boy, don't give yourself any discomfort about the slander of a professional newspaper liar — we can*not* escape such things. I do assure you that this thing did not distress me, or even disturb the flow of my talk (got it at breakfast some days ago), for one single half of a half of a hundredth part of a second; in the same length of time it went out of my mind & was forgotten. To take notice of it in print is a thing which would never have occurred to me. Why, my dear friend, flirt it out of your mind — straight off.

Your [*sic*] truly
S L Clemens

After the spring of 1885 relations between Cable and Twain dwindled very nearly to the vanishing point. Obviously, Cable never lost his respect and affection for Twain; and the evidence indicates that in time Twain's special animus diminished and his memory of pleasant aspects of the relationship took on warm colors. The two novelists exchanged books and met on a cordial basis at occasional literary or social functions. There was no reason for real intimacy. Twain had got from Cable as much perhaps as he could well absorb of Cable's liberal, logical attitudes towards the New South; probably Cable did not have the kind of talent that would profit by contact with Twain, much as he admired him as a person. That Cable did admire Twain he made evident publicly in 1896 and in 1905. In 1896 he printed in the small magazine that he was editing a highly laudatory article on Twain: Literature *may* inform and educate us, he wrote, but it *must* entertain us. Great books are those that can be taken up again and again, and Twain's books meet this requirement. In Twain we have a great humorist who offers the wisdom of truth and art.[76] In 1905 Cable attended the brilliant seventieth birthday celebration given Twain at Delmonico's and was one of the old friends who rose to express affection.[77]

The few letters that are extant from the period after 1885 are polite, friendly, but indicative of a loss of real interest, at least on the part of Twain.

Hartford, June 11/89.

My Dear Cable —

They are lost! I have searched everywhere & cannot find a vestige of that pamphlet. I possess not a single book which I would not sooner have parted with.

We are just leaving for Elmira for the summer. In haste, Ys Sincerely,

S L Clemens

Northampton, Mass., Jan. 6, 1890

Dear Clemens:

I have asked my publishers — I say "my" because, as you know, we authors own the publishers — to send you a copy of my Strange True Stories of Louisiana.[78] If you think it your duty to attack it in the newspapers please do so anonymously, and put your jeers in Roman caps.

We are having a royal time over the Yankee at the Court of King Arthur,[79] which we all thank you for in one breath.

Yours truly
G. W. Cable

Northampton, Mass., Feb'y 1, 1890

Dear Mark:

A sweet girl over in, and native to, England, and who loves you and is afraid you will find it out, is begging me for an autograph letter from you. Mrs. Cable has been looking over my old bunches of letters, but you have had so few occasions to write me that she has not come across one from you. Did you get my book — "Strange True Stories" which I sent you the other day? If so say so in just a line. Isn't the binding pretty? Say that, and I'll send the pronouncement to the English maiden and there'll be at least two of us happier than before.

Yours truly
G. W. Cable

Elmira, June 25/95

Dear Cable:

You make me feel ever so proud & pleased. I wrote the story[80] from love, & one particularly likes to have one's pets praised.

Yes *sir*! I liked you in spite of your religion; & I always said to myself that a man that could be good & kindly with that kind of a load on him was entitled to homage — & I *paid* it. And I have always said, & still maintain, that as a railroad-comrade you were perfect — the only railroad-comrade in the world that a man of moods & frets & uncertainties of disposition could travel with, a third of a year, and never weary of his company. We *always* had good times in the cars & never minded the length of the trips — & my, but they *were* sockdolagers for length!

I was right-down glad to hear from you again.

Sincerely yours,
Mark.

Riverdale, New York City Oct. 15/01

Dear Cable:

Your book[81] came three days ago, your note this morning. I finished reading the story night before last. From start to finish it kept me electrically a-tingle with its rush & go, & charmed with its brilliances of phrasing & its other manifold fascinations. Thank you cordially!

Sincerely yours,
Mark.

Riverdale, New York City, Jan. 9. [1901][82]

Dear Cable:

As regards the Boston book of twelve stories,[83] to which you and I and twenty-three other writers have been advertised as having been invited to contribute, will you mind answering in the respective blanks these following questions, which in all courtesy I ask:

1. Were you invited to contribute?

[Answer: To the best of my recollection and belief, I was]

111

2. Did you contribute? [I have an overpowering conviction that I did.[84]

G. W. Cable]

And may I ask you to return this sheet to me?

Sincerely Yours

MARK TWAIN

[P.S.

Deponent protesteth against having to surrender the inquirer's autograph. What doth the deponent make on this occasion?

G.W.C.]

Bowdoin College Brunswick, Maine, June [21][85], 1904

Dear Mark Twain:

I have heard tardily of your unutterable loss.[86] I know no words with which to comfort your anguish and can only say, I am one who suffers with you, knowing the uncountable value of her who has been taken from you, and your lifelong worship of her.

May the God, in whose wisdom and loving care her faith so perfectly abode somehow empower you to bear the burden of living on as she would exhort you to if she could call back from where she is gone.

Yours truly,

G. W. CABLE

Northampton, MASS., Oct. 31, 1906.

Dear Mark Twain:

This will be brought to you by Mrs. Hazen[87] wife of Professor Hazen,[88] (chair of history Smith College), herself a Smith College alumna.

Mrs. Hazen has an errand to you from the college, and if you are resolved in advance not to respond favorably it would be best not to see her, for if you do you will either change your mind or shatter it.

Yours truly,

G.W.CABLE

FOOTNOTES

INTRODUCTION—FOOTNOTES

1   Lucy L. C. Bikle, *George W. Cable: His Life and Letters* (New York: Charles Scribner's Sons, 1928), p. 69.

2   Under this title, chapters from what became *Life on the Mississippi* began appearing in the *Atlantic Monthly* in January, 1875.

3   See Kjell Ekström, "Cable's *Grandissimes* and the Creoles," *Studia Neophilologica*, XXI (1948-49), 190.

4   Bikle, p. 72, n. In a letter of October 2, 1881, Howells called *The Grandissimes* a "noble and beautiful book, including all the range of tragedy and comedy." He also praised Cable in a letter of March 18, 1882, to John Hay as the "lovliest and loyalest exrebel that lives." Mildred Howells, ed., *Life in Letters of William Dean Howells* (Garden City, New York: Doubleday, Doran and Co., Inc., 1928), I, 301-302; 312.

5   I have tried to avoid unnecessarily duplicating information already available in such places as A. B. Paine, ed., *Mark Twain's Letters* (New York: Harper and Brothers, 1917); Paine, *Mark Twain: A Biography* (New York: Harper and Brothers, 1912); and Dixon Wecter, ed., *The Love Letters of Mark Twain* (New York: Harper and Brothers, 1949).

6   *Letters*, I, 96. Paine mentions one earlier address, perhaps in 1855, in Keokuk, Iowa, at a printer's banquet. *Biography*, I, 107.

7   *Biography*, I, 385; II, 612; and *Letters*, I, 125, 311.

8   *Letters*, I, 416-417.

9   See the headnote to this letter, p. 82, below. For a full account of the address, see my essay "The First Public Address of George W. Cable, Southern Liberal," *Studies in Memory of Frank Martindale Webster* (Washington University Studies, n. s., XX; St. Louis, 1951), pp. 67-76. Cable had addressed church and Sunday School audiences earlier, but he considered this occasion his real debut.

10   Cable's appearances in Baltimore and in Hartford are treated in my article "George W. Cable Becomes a Professional Reader," *American Literature*, XXIII (January, 1952), 467-470. Also see, below, letters of March 7, 1883-March 23, 1883.

11   On November 22, 1883, in Springfield, Massachusetts. Bikle, p. 108.

12   *Century*, VII (January, 1885), 409-419.

13   London, July 3, 1899. Berg Collection, New York Public Library.

14   *Letters*, II, 692.

15   In his reminiscences Pond wrote conventionally and with restraint both of the tour and of Twain's attitude toward Cable. *Eccentricities of Genius* (London: Chatto and Windus, 1901), pp. 227-231, 491-493.

16   There has been a particular lack of agreement about the salary paid to Cable, even by those who should know. Kate O'Leary, in Mary Lawton's *A Life Time with Mark Twain* (New York: Harcourt, Brace and Co., 1925), p. 77, thought that Cable received $500.00 a week. Pond, in *Eccentricities of Genius*, p. 231, set the salary at $600.00. Twain, writing in 1907, put it at $600.00. See Bernard DeVoto, ed., *Mark Twain in Eruption* (New York: Harper and Brothers, 1940), p. 216. Paine gave the figure correctly as $450.00 in the *Biography*, II, 784.

17   Letter from Pond to Cable, June 18, 1884. Cable Collection, Tulane University.

18   Cable Collection, Tulane University.

19   Cable Collection, Tulane University.

20   Samuel Charles Webster, ed., *Mark Twain, Business Man* (Boston: Little, Brown and Co., 1946), pp. 268-270.

21   Webster, pp. 270-271.

22   *Ibid.*, p. 271.

23   *Ibid.*, p. 282.

24   *Love Letters*, p. 230.

25   When they read in Winona, Minnesota, Madison and Milwaukee, Wisconsin, and Davenport, Iowa.

26   When they read in Chicago and Detroit, and in South Bend, Lafayette, and Indianapolis, Indiana.

27   Webster, p. 303. These figures tally very closely with those given by J. B. Pond in his letter of February 2 to Cable, p. 53 below.

28   *Biography*, II, 785.

29   *Mark Twain in Eruption*, pp. 217-223. In an address that he delivered in 1906, Clemens included a sketchy version of the same story. *Mark Twain's Speeches* (New York: Harper and Brothers, 1910), pp. 301-303.
The selections read by Cable were derived (in order as named) from *Dr. Sevier*, Chs. 35, 35, 45, and 54. Twain's "King Sollermun," "How Come a Frenchman Doan' Talk Like a Man?" and the description of the freeing of Jim were taken from *Huckleberry Finn*, Chs. 14, 14, and 35-40. "The Tragic Tale of a Fishwife" and "Difficulties with the German Language" came from Appendix D to *A Tramp Abroad*. "A Trying Situation" was the title Twain gave his story of the young lady at Lucerne, also from *A Tramp Abroad*, Ch. 25. "A Desperate Encounter with an Interviewer" (or, "An Encounter with an Interviewer") appeared first in *Punch, Brothers, Punch!* (New York: Slote, Woodman,

116

and Co., 1878). I have not identified the yarn about Governor Gardiner, Twain's particular version of how the stammerer was cured by whistling, or a printed version of the story of the golden arm (or death pennies), generally announced simply as "A Ghost Story."

30 *Love Letters*, p. 366. The program at Springfield was experimental. Cable started with "Music of Place Congo"; Twain gave "Reminiscences of Artemus Ward"; Cable followed with four selections from "Posson Jone' "; and Twain ended with "The Captain Explains a Difficult Point," "The College Student Sailor," and "Why I Resigned the Editorship." *Republican* (Springfield), November 7, 1884.

31 *Mark Twain in Eruption*, pp. 215-217. Twain was not alone in complaining that the lecture field was dead. Pond made similar complaints, although his view was sometimes optimistic. The Detroit *Free Press* for February 15, 1885, remarked under the heading "Lecturing Played Out" that Henry Ward Beecher cancelled a lecture in New York because the small audience made the occasion "a mortifying failure."

32 *Transcript* (Boston), November 14, 1884.

33 Clara Clemens, *My Father, Mark Twain* (New York: Harper and Brothers, 1931), p. 51. After Twain's death Howells recorded his admiration for him as a performer even more fully:
"He was such a practised speaker that he knew all the stops of that simple instrument man. . . . He was the most consummate public performer I ever saw, and it was an incomparable pleasure to hear him lecture; on the platform he was the great and finished actor which he probably would have been on the stage." *My Mark Twain* (New York: Harper and Brothers, 1901), pp. 51-52.

34 *Daily Advertiser*, November 15, 1884.

35 Twain mentioned to Webster in a letter written from Providence that Edward Windsor Kemble, whom Twain had "discovered" for the *Century*, was being sent by Richard Watson Gilder, the editor, to New Orleans to do illustrations for "a long article" by Cable. Webster, p. 282. Kemble illustrated "The Dance in the Place Congo," XXXI (February, 1886), 517-531, and "Creole Slave Songs," XXI (April, 1886), 807-828. Kemble also did sketches for essays by Eugene V. Smalley on the New Orleans Exposition in the *Century* volume for 1885.

36 Webster, p. 283.

37 *Biography*, II, 799-802. In *Mark Twain's Autobiography* (New York: Harper and Brothers, 1924), I, 32, and II, 59, Paine prints slightly different stories; and a still different account appears in *Mark Twain in Eruption*, p. 170.

38 Bikle, p. 133.

39 *Ibid.*, pp. 133-134.

40 Dean Sage, a particular friend of Twain's was a prominent lumberman, philanthropist, and bibliophile.

41 *Love Letters,* p. 219.

42 Bikle, p. 134.

43 *Idem.*

44 *Biography,* II, 786. Paine repeats the wave imagery that Cable uses.

45 Dixon Wecter mistakenly writes: "Mark Twain always had his moments of self-distrust, but this story suggests even more strongly the envy which his less popular traveling companion could not help feeling on many an occasion." *Love Letters,* pp. 231-232. Cable may have invented the story for any of a number of reasons, but I have found no published evidence of jealousy on his part, and many evidences of admiration. Twain's manic-depressive tendency should not be disregarded.

46 Not Thanksgiving Eve, as Paine supposes in the *Biography,* II, 787.

47 Reproduced in *Biography,* II, 788.

48 *Love Letters,* p. 366.

49 Bikle, p. 135.

50 *Biography,* II, 786-787; and *Love Letters,* p. 221.

51 *Mark Twain Quarterly,* IV (Summer-Fall, 1941), 2.

52 Bikle, p. 135.

53 Cable sometimes found it necessary to go through extraordinary intellectual gyrations in order to accommodate his more worldly activities to his pious principles. On November 8, 1883, he wrote to his wife: "I don't fancy this reading business overmuch. It looks too much like working merely to get money, & that hasn't been my way. I shouldn't feel so, I suppose, for I shall greatly increase the sale of my books, & I do think my books ought to do good. It also lets me into the lecture field. For example the lecture I propose to give to the XIX Cent'y Club is just what I think it a Christian's duty to say to just such a lot of free thinkers & doubters as I am told that club principally comprises." Bikle, p. 107. Under Twain's tutelage Cable's evangelical Protestant qualms subsided, and he learned to speak placidly of his readings as "highway robbery" and "raids on the public treasury."

54 G. E. Jensen, "The Life and Letters of H. C. Bunner," unpublished; cited from Rosa Lee Walton, "A Critical Study of George W. Cable" (Unpublished dissertation, Duke University, 1931), pp. 34-35.

55 Webster, p. 283.

56 Bikle, p. 136.

57 Webster, p. 289.

58 *Love Letters,* p. 224.

59　I have taken a number of facts concerning the tour from a typescript "Extracts from the Diary of Ozias W. Pond" in the Cable Collection, Tulane University.

60　Bikle, p. 138.

61. *Love Letters*, p. 234.

62　Twain wrote to Charley Webster from Keokuk on January 15: "Pond? I will fill no engagement after Feb. 28. I have said it already some 500,000 times." Webster, p. 291.

63　Cable Collection, Tulane University.

64　*Love Letters*, p. 225

65　*Biography*, II, 792.

66　"Mark Twain (Samuel L. Clemens) and George W. Cable (his own name) are associated together in literary entertainments, and will soon strike St. Louis in the hope of making a bit. Sam Clemens is a St. Louis boy, and a Lower Mississippi river pilot, and Cable is a story-teller of New Orleans, who has made a name bigger than the town 'itself.' "

67　Especially in the undeniably offensive essays (even if their accuracy were not in question) in the *Century* for January, February, March, June, and July, 1883, and in the book version of these essays, *The Creoles of Louisiana* (New York: Scribners and Co., 1884).

68　Dictionaries now trace the origin of "Creole" to Latin *creare,* to breed. *Webster's New International Dictionary,* first edition, called the word a corruption of a Spanish diminutive of *criado,* servant, and *A New English Dictionary* mentions this as a possibility. I do not know why Cable thought that the root was the Latin *colere.*

Cable's purpose in his remarks on the word "Creole" seems to have been to pacify the numerous southerners of French or Spanish stock, who, proud of the name, held that Cable implied that Creoles are of mixed white and Negro blood and thus slandered them. Despite the outraged protests of such Louisianians as Charles Gayarré, the fact is that usage has varied widely, even in Louisiana. See, especially, *A Dictionary of American English.*

69　Webster, p. 291.

70　Robert Jones Burdette (1844-1914) was perhaps considered even more a local product than was Twain, although not a native of the region. For nine years he wrote a bi-weekly feature for the Burlington *Daily Hawkeye* which earned that paper a national circulation. Very popular as a lyceum performer, he gave "The Rise and Fall of the Moustache" nearly five thousand times. He became famous, also, as a Baptist preacher in California.

71　*Biography*, II, 792.

72　*Love Letters*, pp. 228-229.

73 Webster, p. 292.

74 *Ibid.*, p. 289.

75 *Ibid.*, p. 293.

76 *Love Letters*, pp. 230-231.

77 Information on the stay in Minneapolis and St. Paul comes from E. F. Pabody, "Mark Twain's Ghost Story," *Minnesota History*, XVIII (March, 1937), 28-35.

78 Excerpts from the *Wisconsin State Journal* (Madison) are cited from Fred W. Lorch, "Cable and His Reading Tour with Mark Twain in 1884-1885," *American Literature*, XXIII (January, 1952), 477-478, 485-486.

79 Cable Collection, Tulane University.

80 Cable Collection, Tulane University.

81 *Love Letters*, p. 229.

82 Webster, p. 283.

83 *Love Letters*, p. 229. "Le Desirous" is from Malory.

84 Bikle, p. 132, n; and Fred W. Lorch, "Lecture Trips and Visits of Mark Twain in Iowa," *Iowa Journal of History and Politics*, XXVII (October, 1929), 534.

85 Edward Larocque Tinker, "Cable and the Creoles," *American Literature*, V (January, 1934), 322.

86 *Love Letters*, p. 234.

87 *Ibid.*, p. 235.

88 *Ibid.*, pp. 234-235.

89 *Ibid.*, pp. 235-236.

90 *Ibid.*, p. 236.

91 Russel B. Nye presents supporting evidence in "Mark Twain in Oberlin," *Ohio State Archaeological and Historical Quarterly*, XLVII (January, 1938), 69-73. I argue against this supposition in "Mark Twain's Hadleyburg," *Ohio State Archaeological and Historical Quarterly*, LX (July, 1951), 257-264.

92 *Tuque* is Canadian French for *toque*.

93 *Letters*, II, 449-450.

94 Bikle, pp. 139-141; *Love Letters*, p. 238.

95 Twain wrote "Brockton," but he must have meant "Brockville," on a letter of February 17 to Charley Webster. Webster, p. 304.

96 *Love Letters*, p. 237.

97 *Gazette* (Montreal), February 17, 1885. "Mr. Charlton" was the Honorable John Charlton (1829-1910), born in the state of New York and known as an advocate of commercial union with the United States. "Sir John" was the veteran Prime Minister, Sir John Alexander Mac-

donald (1815-1891).

98 Words and music are given in the *Century*, XXI (April, 1886), 825-826.

99 Bikle, pp. 141-143. Cable kept up the acquaintance with Iles. He presented him with a photograph of himself on February 19 and received letters and books from him in later years. See correspondence, Ms Division, Library of Congress.

100 *Letters*, II, 450.

101 J. B. Pond notes that Cable occupied more time on the platform than Clemens thought the audience approved, but it is not obvious that either Pond or the audience agreed with Twain. *Eccentricities of Genius*, p. 227. By pragmatic tests Cable's reputation for effectiveness as speaker and reader is secure. Newspaper critics praised him almost as warmly as they did Twain, and for more than twenty years he made a substantial part of his living on the platform. He was, I think, not in the same class with Twain, but few men have been. At the beginning of his career his manner was simple but effective, according to a number of published reports. See, for example, the *American and Commercial Advertiser* (Baltimore), March 20, 1883, which described his manner as natural and free from artifices of every sort; see, also, Charles Dudley Warner, who wrote that Cable interpreted his own writings by a method "so simple and without pretense as to seem to lack art." *Century*, IV (June, 1883), 311-312. His light tenor voice did lack carrying power; and he worked with two different teachers of elocution between 1883 and 1886, primarily to develop strength of voice. The danger of artificiality was one that he recognized, and he and his second teacher rejoiced at newspaper notices that claimed for him a naturalness and grace quite different from professional art and "better than anything he could have acquired *by months* of elocutionary training." Bikle, p. 146.

102 November 21, 1883. Howells Collection, Harvard University.

103 *My Mark Twain*, p. 53.

104 Clara Clemens, p. 52.

105 May 5, 1885. Original in Berg Collection, New York Public Library; copy in Howells Collection, Harvard University.

106 June 5, 1885. Howells Collection, Harvard University.

107 *Mark Twain in Eruption*, pp. 215-216.

108 June 25, 1895. Cable Collection, Tulane University. The same passage is quoted with minor changes in Bikle, p. 197, n.

109 See, below, the correspondence dated May, 1885.

110 *Biography*, II, 784.

111 Bikle, p. 144. It may be noted that much earlier in his career Cable had been lukewarm in his admiration for Twain's writings. In his "Drop Shot" column, published in the *Picayune* (New Orleans) in

1870, he preferred Josh Billings to Twain. Arlin Turner, "George Washington Cable's Literary Apprenticeship," *Louisiana Historical Quarterly*, XXIV (January, 1941), 168-170.

112 He was so much in the public eye that almost any triviality that could be attached to his name was worth a story. For example, the following item was reprinted from the *News* (Philadelphia) by the *Times-Democrat* (New Orleans) for December 29, 1884:

"Mr. Clemens has some peculiarities. They tell me he is one of the most nervous men in the world. He has constant difficulty in keeping still, and somebody is obliged to go with him to keep him busy playing billiards or doing something else, so that he will not have to be faced with the horrible alternative of sitting still."

This same newspaper story explained that Twain always reserved one seat in the drawing room and one in the smoking compartment and shuttled back and forth between them, unable to stand smoke unless he was smoking himself.

113 The divergent accounts given by Paine, Twain, and Cable tally moderately well at key points. See *Biography*, II, 790; Paine, ed., *Mark Twain's Notebook* (New York: Harper and Brothers, 1935), p. 171; and Bikle, pp. 143-144, n. The incident must have taken place in Rochester, New York, on Saturday, December 6, 1884.

114 Bernard DeVoto, *Mark Twain at Work*, (Cambridge, Massachusetts: Harvard University Press, 1942), p. 85.

115 Mr. DeVoto (*loc. cit.*) believes that Cable took to be improperly suggestive the title of one of Twain's readings "in which, after solemn thought," he cannot make out what Cable had in mind. The title questioned was, "Can't Learn a Nigger to Argue." Cable's phrasing was obscure; nevertheless, I suppose that he was protesting the use of the word "nigger" out of dramatic context. See Cable's letter of October 25, 1884, p. 105 below.

116 Departures from the extant manuscript are discussed, with some difference of opinion, by Bernard DeVoto and DeLancey Ferguson. See, especially, DeVoto, *Mark Twain at Work*, pp. 82-85; Ferguson, "Huck Finn A-Borning," *Colophon*, n.s., III (Spring, 1938), 171-180; and Ferguson, *Mark Twain: Man and Legend* (Indianapolis and New York: Bobbs-Merrill and Co., 1943), pp. 219-227.

117 *Autobiography*, II, 89-90.

118 Webster, pp. 271-272; *Mark Twain at Work*, p. 82.

119 Bikle, pp. 90, 96-97, 116-118.

120 His intellectual and emotional development forms a crucial problem for the serious student of Twain's work; yet there is lacking a systematic study tracing historically changes in outlook that took place during his life in the West, in Hawaii, in New England, and in Europe.

121 *Mark Twain at Work*, p. 89.

122 *Ibid.*, p. 54.

123 *Ibid.*, p. 49, n.

124 DeVoto establishes quite convincingly the major dates of composition. *Ibid.*, pp. 45-104.

125 Bikle, p. 69. On March 7, 1882, Howells wrote to Cable that he and Twain were so taken with *The Grandissimes* that they "went about talking Creole all day." Kjell Ekström, "The Cable-Howells Correspondence," *Studia Neophilologica*, XXII (1949-50), 53.

126 This and the immediately following quotations are from editorials in the Atlanta *Constitution* for November 3 and 30, 1879. Cited from Gregory Paine, ed., *Southern Prose Writers* (New York: American Book Co., 1947), pp. 269-271.

127 Howells remembered Twain as a reader (on other occasions) of both Harris and Cable: "No one could read *Uncle Remus* like him; his voice echoed the voices of the negro nurses who told his childhood the wonderful tales. I remember especially his raptures with Mr. Cable's *Old Creole Days*, and the thrilling force with which he gave the forbidding of the leper's brother when the city's survey ran the course of an avenue through the cottage where the leper lived in hiding: 'Strit must not pass!' " *My Mark Twain*, pp. 99-100.

128 November 4, 1882, in *Letters*, I, 426-427.

129 *Mark Twain at Work*, pp. 54-55.

130 *Biography*, II, 754.

131 Bikle, p. 117.

132 Howells called Twain "the most desouthernized Southerner" he ever knew and added, to make his meaning clear: "No man more perfectly sensed and more entirely abhorred slavery, and no one has ever poured such scorn upon the second-hand, Walter-Scotticized, pseudo-chivalry of the Southern ideal." *My Mark Twain*, p. 35.

LETTERS—FOOTNOTES

1   *Madame Delphine.* Scribner's published this story, one of Cable's best, serially (in *Scribner's Monthly,* May, June, July) and in book form in 1881. It was reprinted, together with other stories, by Frederick Warne and Co., London, at about the same time that it appeared as a separate volume in New York. Cable received a copy of the English reprint on July 2. Bikle, *George W. Cable,* p. 71.

2   The incurably diffident Joel Chandler Harris.

3   James R. Osgood, the publisher, Twain's companion on his Mississippi River excursion in the spring of 1882.

4   There are seven listings of the name Guthrie in the New Orleans *City Directory* for 1882. Twain spent one evening at the home of a Mr. Guthrie, who was "the brother of David Gray's wife." Wecter, ed., *Love Letters,* p. 212. David Gray (1836-88), editor of the *Courier* (Buffalo), married Martha Terry Guthrie, of New Orleans.

5   Mrs. Antoinette Cable Cox, a sister of Cable's with whom his mother lived at 226 Eighth Street, across the street from Cable.

6   One of Mrs. Cox's three children.

7   *The Stolen White Elephant,* just printed by Osgood and Co. Copyright copies were filed on June 12, 1882.

8   Jean, born July 26, 1880.

9   For a full treatment of this address, see my essay "The First Public Address of George W. Cable, Southern Liberal," *op. cit.* It must be noted that evidence of the hostility of Cable's audience depends primarily on the memories of three auditors fifty years after the event. See David H. Bishop, "A Commencement in the Eighties," *Southwest Review,* XVIII (1933), 108-114.

10   According to a letter that Clemens wrote to John Garth, a friend of his Hannibal boyhood, Jean did have scarlet fever, Susy was ill with some other disease, and Clemens himself was "stretched on the bed with three diseases at once, and all of them fatal." Paine, ed., *Mark Twain's Letters,* I, 422-423.

11   Twain later referred to *The Stolen White Elephant* as "rubbishy sketches, mainly." DeVoto, ed., *Mark Twain in Eruption,* p. 158.

12   Antoinette Cox.

13   Office of the *Century Magazine.*

14   Cable wrote "Clements" before correcting the name to "Clemens."

15   Either Charles Dudley Warner or, possibly, George Warner, both of them neighbors and close friends.

16   Joseph Hopkins Twichell, minister of a fashionable Congregational church and a very dear friend of Clemens.

17   *Life on the Mississippi,* manufactured by Osgood and Company,

was published in May, 1883, by subscription, with Charles L. Webster, husband of Clemens' niece, Annie Moffett, acting as subscription manager.

18   Bikle, p. 90.

19   Probably the George Warners.

20   The Reverend Edwin P. Parker, pastor of the South Congregational Church, Hartford.

21   Seven Cheneys but no Cheeneys are listed in the Hartford *City Directory*. This is probably the son-in-law of Horace Bushnell.

22   Either Samuel C. Dunham, a lawyer and insurance man who was a friend of Twain's, or Austin C. Dunham, one of those who helped promote Cable's first reading in Hartford. Both were at this time members of the firm of A. D. Dunham and Sons.

23   Joseph Hawley, a Civil War general, editor of the *Daily Courant*, politician, and governor of Connecticut.

24   Many of Twain's friends in Hartford belonged to this Monday Evening Club, which met on alternate Mondays from October to May for reading papers and for discussion.

25   The familiar salutations here, in the following letter and in a few other places, appear to have been initiated by Cable. In his letters to others Clemens was not sportively inclined in just this way, and the humor of this mode of address seems to have palled very quickly on him.

26   Postal card.

27   *Life on the Mississippi.*

28   Twain wrote on the edge of the envelope: "No Stuart in the lot, but give me the full title & I'll rob a library for you."

29   Postal card.

30   The friendship between Smith and Cable was a cordial one. At Smith's death Cable wrote and published privately a small commemorative volume called *A Memory of Roswell Smith* (New York, [1892]).

31   Charles Dudley Warner.

32   The invitation is reprinted in Bikle, pp. 94-95, n.

33   A "ticket" for the lecture was published in New York and Hartford newspapers. *Ibid.*, p. 95.

34   On March 29 Cable wrote from New York to his wife of working "straight along" on his Hartford "lecture." Perhaps he meant "reading," or he may have decided after the twenty-ninth to read rather than to lecture, Bikle, p. 95.

35   Cable Collection, Tulane University.

36   In New York. Cable, after attending a meeting of the "Authors' Club" on the night of March 28 at the home of E. C. Stedman, gave in a letter home a partial list of those present: Roswell Smith, John Albee,

Joaquin Miller, Charles DeKay, George P. Lathrop, H. C. Bunner, J. Brander Matthews, Richard Grant White, Julian Hawthorne, and R. W. Gilder. Bikle, p. 95.

37   Tomasso Salvini, the Italian actor, made a great splash during his stay in the United States, 1880-84. Cable, who was wrestling with his conscience about the morality of attending the theater, refused to see him. He wrote regretfully later to his wife of missing "the immortal Salvini." *Ibid.*, pp. 101-102.

38   Twain often read to the Saturday Morning Club, a group of Hartford women.

39   For Cable's mother and sister.

40   Of Drake and Parsons, bookbinders, publishers, and general book manufacturers, 354 Asylum Street, Hartford.

41   Clemens visited the Marquis of Lorne, Governor-General of Canada, and his wife, the Princess Louise. Paine, *Biography*, II, 748-749.

42   For *Life on the Mississippi*.

43   Clemens never forgave Elisha Bliss for supposed injuries. Paine, *Biography*, II, 696-697; Webster, ed., *Mark Twain, Business Man*, *passim*; and DeVoto, ed., *Mark Twain in Eruption*, pp. 148 ff.

44   They went to Quarry Farm, where Clemens completed *Huck Finn*.

45   The *Post*, November 22, 1883.

46   On November 29, 1883, and December 5, 1883. The *Post* for December 5 carried a criticism of the third reading which was not entirely favorable.

47   The *Morning Journal*, December 12.

48   Bikle, p. 112.

49   By Wecter (ed.) in *Love Letters*, p. 219. On the joke, see p. 102 below.

50   This point of view is taken by DeVoto (ed.) in *Adventures of Huckleberry Finn* (New York: Limited Editions Club, 1942), p. x.

51   Bikle, p. 118, n. There is a good chance that Mark was right. Cable's nurse had mumps soon after leaving him, and one or more of his children had them before he visited Clemens.

52   March 5, 1884. Howells Collection, Harvard University.

53   October 17, 1884. Howells Collection, Harvard University.

54   The *Press*, January 23, announced that Cable would give two or three of the readings with which he had delighted the people of Boston and New York. The programs would include "African Creole" songs and anecdotes. On the twenty-eighth the paper announced that Cable would be received by the Penn Club.

55   The *Press* for January 29 announced a postponement and reported that Twain had sent word to Pond that Cable had influenza.
Dates for the readings were advanced to February 2 and February 5.
The paper for February 4 reported a telegram from Clemens saying
that Cable had high fever but that hopes were entertained for his re-
covery. On February 19 his first appearance was announced for that
night, and on February 22 the strongly favorable opinion produced at
his first appearance was said to have created a demand for tickets to his
second reading on February 23. The reviewer exhausted his supply of
laudatory adjectives in reporting the reading on the twenty-second.

The *Public Ledger* was equally assiduous and flattering. It announced
on the nineteenth that Cable was considered a clever writer and effective reader "with an advantage over Dickens and Wilkie Collins." On
the twentieth it reported his first reading, "where the culture of the
audience was an honor"; and on February 25 it reported the final reading on the twenty-fourth.

56   Bikle, pp. 116-118.

57   Mrs. George Warner.

58   Paine tells the story of Clemens' interest in Ambulinia, heroine
of a grandiloquent romance called *Love Triumphant, or the Enemy
Conquered.* Joe Twichell discovered "about a cord" of copies that spring
in the basement of a bookstore in New Haven. *Biography,* II, 765-767.

59   Dr. Francis Bacon, of Yale, lent his copy of *Love Triumphant* to
Cable.

60   Writing from the Middle West, "a few weeks later," Cable told
his wife that his doctor said emphatically "no" to his having had mumps.
Bikle, p. 118, n.

61   Probably the George Warners, but the Charles Dudley Warners
may have been included.

62   Paine, *Biography,* II, 769. Webster publishes a rather good letter
from R. W. Raymond in *Mark Twain, Business Man,* p. 247.

63   Bikle, p. 119.

64   The *Tribune* (Chicago), March 23, 25, 29, 30, 1884.

65   *Ibid.,* March 30, 1884.

66   Clemens and Cable were "serious" artists only part of the time.
Often they were merely looking for novelty or a selling feature. This
particular project never came to fruition.

67   Webster, p. 277.

68   For *The Adventures of Huckleberry Finn.* The passage Cable
likes comes at the end of Ch. 8.

69   Colonel George E. Waring, Jr., of Newport, who commissioned
Cable to write on New Orleans for the U. S. Census for 1880. Bikle,
pp. 64-65. Waring wrote an essay on Cable for the *Century Magazine,*
IV (June, 1882), 311-312.

70 *Love Letters,* p. 237.

71 Whether Cable did or did not accede to this request I have not discovered, but he did, of course, give freely of his time to causes which interested him.

72 I give the story of this episode and of its implications in "Mark Twain's 'Row' with George Cable," *Modern Language Quarterly,* XIII (December, 1952), 363-371.

73 Edward Larocque Tinker refers to complaints and epithets in Clemens' letters to Pond in "Cable and the Creoles," *American Literature,* V (January, 1934), 321-322.

74 I have found the story in the *Sunday Herald* (Boston) and in the *Times-Democrat* (New Orleans). Also, as though referring to a well-known quarrel, the *World* (New York) for May 17 regrets that the Twain-Cable combination should be dissolved over so trivial a question as Cable's charging his champagne and boot-blacking to the general expense fund.

75 Telegram.

76 "Samuel L. Clemens. 'Mark Twain,'" *The Letter,* IV (February 1, 1896), 70.

77 Paine, *Biography,* III, 1252.

78 Published in 1889.

79 *A Connecticut Yankee in the Court of King Arthur,* Twain's first book in five years, appeared in December, 1889.

80 *Joan of Arc* was appearing serially in *Harper's Magazine* and was rather generally known to be by Clemens, although he had not acknowledged the authorship publicly.

81 *The Cavalier,* completed in the spring of 1900 after long and strenuous labor and published in 1901, did not live up to the hopes of Cable or the praise of Clemens.

82 This manifolded letter went out to twenty-four writers. Twain wrote in by hand the name of each addressee, and Cable answered in his own hand as indicated by brackets.

83 Paul Leicester Ford, ed., *A House Party* (Boston: Small, Maynard and Co., 1901).

84 Cable contributed "The Angel of the Lord."

85 The envelope is postmarked June 21, 1904. Cable misdated the letter "June 22."

86 Olivia L. Clemens died at Florence, Italy, on June 5, 1904.

87 Sarah Sefton Duryea Hazen. Mrs. Hazen probably invited Clemens to read or lecture.

88 Charles D. Hazen.

LIST of LETTERS

This list includes two postal cards, one telegram, and one jointly written letter. Letters in the Cable Collection at Tulane are marked "T.," and those in the Mark Twain papers belonging to the Mark Twain Estate are marked "M.T.E.," whether originals or copies. Originals, when they can be determined, are marked "orig." The original of the letter of October 14, 1882, is in the possession of S. C. Webster.

Date	Persons	Source	Page
July 17, 1881	Clemens to Cable	T., orig.	81
June 20, 1882	Clemens to Cable	T., orig.	81
June 29, 1882	Cable to Clemens	T.; M.T.E., orig.	83
September 26, 1882	Cable to Clemens	T.; M.T.E., orig.	83
[September 29, 1882?]	Clemens to Cable	T., orig.	84
October 5, 1882	Clemens to Cable	T.	84
October 9, 1882	Cable to Clemens	M.T.E., orig.	85
October 12, 1882	Clemens to Cable	T.	85
October 14, 1882	Cable to Clemens	T.; M.T.E.	86
October 16, 1882	Clemens to Cable	T.	86
November 7, 1882	Cable to Clemens	T.; M.T.E., orig.	87
November 11, 1882	Clemens to Cable	T.	87
January 9, 1883	Cable to Clemens	T.; M.T.E., orig.	89
January 15, 1883	Clemens to Cable	T., orig.	89
January 18, 1883	Cable to Clemens	T.; M.T.E., orig.	89
March 7, 1883	Clemens to Cable	T., orig.	90
[March 17, 1883]	Clemens to Cable	T., orig.	91
March 20, 1883	Cable to Clemens	T.; M.T.E., orig.	91
March 23, 1883	Clemens to Cable	T.	92
April 16, 1883	Clemens to Cable	T.	93
May 22, 1883	Cable to Clemens	T.; M.T.E., orig.	94
June 4, 1883	Clemens to Cable	T.	95
February 1, 1884	Mrs. Clemens to Mrs. Cable	T., orig.	97
February 2, 1884	Mrs. George Warner to Mrs. Cable	T., orig.	98

Date	Persons	Source	Page
February 3, 1884	Clemens to Pond	T., orig.	99
February 6, 1884	Mrs. Clemens to Mrs. Cable	T., orig.	99
February 7, 1884	Mrs. Clemens Mrs. Cable	T., orig.	99
February 16, 1884	Pond and Cable to Clemens	M.T.E., orig.	100
February 18, 1884	Cable to Clemens	M.T.E., orig.	101
February 21, 1884	Cable to Clemens	T.; M.T.E., orig.	101
March 29, 1884	Cable to Clemens	T.; M.T.E., orig.	103
April 15, 1884	Cable to Clemens	T.; M.T.E., orig.	103
September 10, 1884	Cable to Clemens	M.T.E., orig.	104
October 13, 1884	Cable to Clemens	T.; M.T.E., orig.	104
October 25, 1884	Cable to Clemens	M.T.E., orig.	104
March 2, 1885	Mrs. Clemens to to Cable	T., orig.	107
May 15, 1885	Cable to Clemens	M.T.E., orig.	108
May 16, 1885	Cable to Clemens	T.; M.T.E., orig.	108
[May 18, 1885?]	Clemens to Cable	T., orig.	109
June 11, 1889	Clemens to Cable	T., orig.	110
January 6, 1890	Cable to Clemens	T.; M.T.E., orig.	110
February 1, 1890	Cable to Clemens	M.T.E., orig.	110
June 25, 1895	Clemens to Cable	T., orig.	111
October 15, 1901	Clemens to Cable	T., orig.	111
January 9, [1901]	Clemens to Cable	T.; M.T.E., orig.	111
June [21], 1904	Cable to Clemens	T.; M.T.E., orig.	112
October 31, 1906	Cable to Clemens	T.; M.T.E., orig.	112

INDEX of PERSONS